CONTEN⁻

THE FEMALE PSYCHOLOGY

Men and Women are different. Period. The idea of equality when it comes to sex is merely a concept and, as much as we'd all love for it to exist, it doesn't – there are biological differences and limits when it comes to sex. These differences don't only exist physically, but also, and perhaps more prominently, psychologically.

This is a truth and is a truth that both men and women need to accept when it comes to their sex lives – if we want to understand each other sexually, we first need to accept and understand the differences. Once you are able to attain such an understanding, you will be able to become a better lover in and out of bed; you will be better able to sexually satisfy your partner.

The female psychology, when it comes to sex, stems from evolution. As human beings, we are designed to reproduce sexually and it is our innate drive to have sex that makes us successful. Men produce endless quantities of sperm on a daily basis over the course of their entire life. Women, on the other hand, produce eggs. The production of eggs requires an extraordinary amount of energy in comparison to the production of sperm, and only occurs once per month.

Evolutionarily speaking, given that men produce so much sperm over their lifetimes, they need as many sexual partners as possible in order to better guarantee the passing of their sperm and the birth of their own children with the aim to secure their genetic data for the next generation. This is the root of the male psychology towards sex. Women, on the other hand, again from an evolutionary perspective, have to goal of finding a mate to physically take care of her and her children – women look to secure the best man possible to achieve this.

This is all fairly straightforward, but it is the understanding of the implication of this basic biology that will allow you to begin learning how to have a better sex life. As you can imagine, the evolutionary differences in sex psychology between men and women will cause a conflict – the two ideals are completely opposite to one-another – men want to have sex and impregnate as many women as possible, and women want to secure one single man to stay with her and take care of her children. So, what has evolution produced to solve this issue? Love.

Now, we all have our own ideas of what love really is and quite often people's interpretation of love as a word is very different. But love is a mechanism of evolution that has developed strongly in the human mind. Love is an attachment, a strong one, which exists through space and time. It is the connection one person has to another and causes them to have undying emotions and urges to protect, take care of and support them. The concept of love is evolution's answer to the psychological differences between the sexes and works in favour of the female mind when it comes to sex and reproduction. Love produces loyalty in men towards their female partner and impedes their biological drive to find and impregnate lots of women.

The ultimate goal of love is to ensure and uphold such a loyalty to one woman. A child takes years to develop physically until they are in a position to take care of themselves and, to survive, they need to be nurtured. The woman in this reproductive cycle is unable to do this herself and requires a man to provide food, shelter, and general security for her and the child. This cycle can be put quite simply in terms of bargaining. The woman is biologically required in order to reproduce and take care of children. In return for protection, the man is rewarded with a child and secures his genetic data for the next generation.

It is clear by this point the value of sex to us all, men and women, as human beings. Sex is a key part of our psychology, and although the female psychology is directed more so in the way of love, women want sex. Despite the biological urge to be extremely selective when it comes to finding a man, women retain a high sex drive in order to drive them to find a mate as soon as she can, given that sexual fertility peaks at a younger age for women and they are limited to their window of opportunity to reproduce – most women reach menopause around their 50s and are thereafter unable to have children.

This may all seem very straightforward, but it is by truly understanding this process which will allow you to improve your sex life. You will be able to use the sexual psychology of women to work in your favour.

THE VALUE OF SEX

Sex is clearly valuable to men and women. You know that, I know that, everybody knows. But what a shocking amount of people understand about the value of sex is confused and inaccurate. Most men assume that women want what they want and that the value of sex is the same for both men and women, but is really isn't.

I'm not telling you that women don't want sex. They do. And they want it just as much as men. In fact, studies of students at universities have found that the desire to have casual sex is an equal 50/50 split between the male and female populations. Of course, there are cultural differences and other variables to consider, but this is generally true. What is different, however, is the way in which women express their sexual desires.

In Western societies, you need to understand that there are barriers when it comes to sex. Societal barriers. Physical barriers. Cultural barriers. Barriers which have led to the value of sex to differ between the genders – some things are acceptable in society when it comes to having sex with people, and some things are simply unacceptable. To understand this is key. It is the only way to have success attracting women, having sex with women, and satisfying them sexually.

Now, up until now, I've maintained a strong theme on

evolution. There's a reason for this. A lot of people neglect the reasoning behind behaviour. Sure, we all want to have sex because it feels great. But there's more to it and if you really want to have success when it comes to finding a woman, you need to remember this. Whenever you read about sex or having sex yourself, you need to remember that there is far more to it than just having a good time. Women value sex because sex attracts men, and men provide them with security. They want to be able to trust this man in the long-term and use him to protect her investments – her eggs, and ultimately, her children. Men, on the other hand, don't have such big investments – no man ever needs to worry about protecting his sperm because it is created rapidly and constantly. The differences between men and women here is reflected in the need for trust. This is why, even if you are only looking for casual sex, you are pretty much going to find it impossible without first developing a level of trust between you and the woman. Think about it. How many times have you had sex? And then think, have I ever had sex without having to spend a considerable amount of time talking to the woman and making her trust me? Probably not. Of course, everybody is different and you might get lucky, but there is an undeniable, underlaying truth that holds strong here.

Trust is a value which women hold highly. They need to be able to trust that the man will be able to provide for her and protect her family. Why do you think that, in general, women find muscular men attractive? Or rich men? Because, from our evolutionary history, muscular men are better able to protect families from the dangers which existed and provide for them by hunting, creating shelter etc. In the modern society, a woman might find a man with money attractive as he will be able to provide those things with money. But the point is, women need to be able to trust that their man can do this for them, otherwise they are virtually worthless to them. The focus on trust here is probably a lot bigger than you would have ever imagined – trust paves way for a huge list of different things women crave when it comes to sex and finding a man; romance being one of the most significant. We'll talk about this later.

6 WAYS TO BECOME MORE CONFIDENT IN BED

One important aspect of attracting any woman is confidence which, unfortunately, is a quality most men lack and most men are afraid to portray. None-the-less, if you ever want to be great in bed, you need it.

The truth is, confidence is a mindset and as such it can be taught. There may be endless reasons why you feel like you shouldn't be confident in bed. You may feel like you haven't had enough experience or you may be self-conscious about your body or that your hitting out of your league, but here I want to talk to you about why this should never be the case no matter who you are.

In my opinion, there are 2 main reasons why you might not have confidence.

1. You are unfamiliar with what it is you need to do, so you get nervous
2. You are afraid of what others think

And yes, the two do go hand-in-hand – you may be unfamiliar with what you need to do which makes you worried about what others think if you do it wrong and you get nervous, ultimately failing. It's like a self-fulfilling prophecy.

I now want to take you through 10 ways that you can train your mind to be confident. Try to really internalise what we talk about here because if you don't develop confidence in yourself, you will never have that confidence in the bedroom and NEVER become great in bed. It all starts here.

And before we begin, I want you to remember that most points made here are actually life skills, they don't have to only be related to sex! Confidence can affect every aspect of our lives and therefore you should try and apply as many of these as possible to ever situation you ever find yourself in – the more confidence you have in your day-to-day life, the more this will be naturally reflected in the bedroom without you even needing to think about it.

1. What's the worst that could happen?

We all know that situations can go from bad to worse and then we're stuck having to deal with something that we could have avoided altogether. It happens. But when it does happen, we need a plan! If you end up doing something and not planning for the outcomes, good or bad, then when they happen, we freeze. We have no idea what to do because we're all generally pretty bad when it comes to thinking on the spot. So, plan. Even if there is a miniscule chance of a negative outcome, you should prepare for it so that if it does happen, you can avoid the negative outcomes that stem from it. Once you do this, you'll feel much more confident because you are ready for whatever may happen. The only way to advance in anything is to take risks and hope they work out so you should never be afraid, just prepared. And remember, in reality, the actual outcome is usually far, far better than the worst-case scenario so don't let it overwhelm you.

2. The Psychology Behind a Lack of Confidence

You can probably guess that a lot of things to do with a lack of confidence stem from our psychology and the way that we think about ourselves. You're right. In fact, confidence is all about psychology. There can be physical triggers i.e. you may lack confidence because you aren't comfortable with your body, but confidence exists in our mind.

Whether you know a lot about psychology, a little bit or nothing at all, I want to talk to you about NATS. NATS are negative automatic thoughts and weigh in heavily on how you see yourself. They operate on both the conscious level and the unconscious level. For example, one NAT could be something like this, 'I'm single because I'm not good looking enough' or 'I'm not good in bed because I can't last long enough'. These thoughts weigh you down constantly whether you know they are there or not and your confidence suffers as a result.

If you ever feel awkward and uncomfortable in any situation, it's probably because you have a thousand different thoughts running around in your mind telling you that you have a reason to feel awkward. If you've ever been on a dance floor and felt completely alienated because you don't think you can dance or you think that other people care about how you're dancing, you know what I'm talking about here. What you need to remember is that this is simply your mind constructing possible events around you and they are NOT real – they simply exist because your mind has been conditioned to respond in this way.

What you need to do is create distance from these NATS. If you ever notice you having a negative thought about yourself, literally force it out of your mind. If you hear in your head 'my skin doesn't look too good today', ignore it and REPLACE it with something positive. Create a habit of doing this and over time your negative automatic thoughts will begin to extinguish themselves before you even know they are there! I promise you, even if this sounds too simple, it's psychology and it works.

Oh, and just a heads up. Now you've read this, you're going to notice NATS a lot more often so get to work!

3. Don't be afraid to act a little until you get going

To begin with, the idea of suddenly becoming a confident person might scare you because that person is going to behave quite differently to the way you act now. And it isn't going to happen overnight, but getting started is usually the biggest challenge.

When you begin aiming for this new you with the confidence to express your actual personality, you might want to start by pretending. The more familiar you get with expressing confidence, even if it is just talking to a cashier in your local shop for example, the more comfortable you are going to get and the more natural it will feel. Eventually, this confidence will be expressed without you even needing to think about it or pretend anymore. Once you've accomplished this, you'll notice how much better you'll feel when you're having sex because it will simply come naturally. This is your goal, right?

4. Accept your past

This is one which might be a little hard to deal with, but I promise you it's an important step that you really cannot skip. Most of what we think about ourselves, including NATS, stem from our history – our past relationships, our experiences in school and pretty much any area of our lives. You can't ignore this.

First, you need to think about all the significant memories you have, good or bad. Think about why they are memories – why is it that in all the things you've done, THAT is what has stuck in your mind. It might be the memory of when you had your first kiss or it might be something completely different like the first time you went on a plane. Think about these times and the emotions you experience, and then try to link it to how it makes you feel now. Have they effected your confidence? Are you nervous around girls because you got humiliated 10 years ago and you never got over it? Whatever it is, you need to accept it and work on reversing any negative outcome that it may have produced. I know it seems a little far-fetched to think that a kiss 10 years ago could affect your sex life now, but you'd be surprised in the power of old memories. Remember, it wouldn't be a memory unless there are some significance to the emotions to felt at the time, and the outcomes of it.

5. Exercise

I know you've probably seen this suggestion on every blog or book you've ever read about confidence. But there is a reason for it. I'm not going to bore you with all the stuff you've heard a thousand times about endorphins and what not, but I will promise you one thing. If you begin working out, your sex life will indefinitely improve in incredible amounts. If you wake up every day and see improvements in your physical self, you will begin to love yourself. Confidence will come naturally. All those NATS will begin to disappear and most likely be replaced by positive ones. Every aspect of your life will improve by following a simple workout regime. And what's more is that once you start and commit to it, you will become addicted! You might hear about how people get addicted to running or hitting the gym, and that really could be you. It will become a hobby and I mean, what could be better than a hobby which improves everything about yourself. Workout and see the benefits in and out of the bedroom.

6. Invest in Yourself

A lot of you will want to dismiss this one, but you shouldn't. You should invest in yourself like there's no tomorrow. Even if you're one of those guys who think 'I don't really care what my hair looks like' or 'These shoes will do', you still need to invest in yourself and stop being stubborn! Even the simplest thing like getting a new, good haircut that you love and a nice pair of jeans or a new jacket could completely change the way you interact with people – you'd be surprised how much difference a new wardrobe can do for you! You'll appreciate yourself more, you'll feel better (and more confident, if you didn't assume so already), and women will respond! If you want to impress a girl you can't just do the same old thing in those trouser you bought 3 years ago and wash once a week. You have the make the effort! She will notice it immediately, be more inclined to spend time with you and see you as a better investment. It's a win-win all round, so do it. Really pay attention to your image. You could run in to a girl at any time, so always be looking good, feeling good, and give yourself more reasons to feel confident. First impressions count.

SEDUCTION MASTERY: THE ART OF SEDUCTION

Seduction is an ambiguous area of sex today. What comes to mind when you hear the word seduction? How does it work? You might be thinking of a suave guy in a suit talking exquisitely over a dinner, or on the other hand, you might be thinking of a muscular man with his top off showing himself off to a girl. The truth is, it doesn't really matter how you seduce someone, as long as it works for them. What is important, however, is the reasons behind seduction.

Like I just said, there are lots of ways women can be seduced, and some are very different than others. You don't need some secret one-line pick up line or be the smoothest lad on the block to get a woman in to bed. Sure, these might work from time to time, but all you need to know is that you aren't limited by or to them.

You should think of seduction as a method of persuasion because, for all intensive purposes, it is! All you are really doing is trying to persuade the woman to sleep with you. Seduction, on a basic level, is merely your method to persuade a woman to have sex with you by taking advantage of her sex drive.

So, how do you seduce a woman? Seduction, although it can be a bit more forward, is about sending the right signals. Unfortunately, this is where most guys will fail – the whole concept of luring someone to a bedroom seems foreign to them, it just simply doesn't make sense to them. But where do they go wrong? Why?

The thing to remember is that seduction can happen anywhere and everywhere. The woman could be sat right next to you, or she could be a million miles away. Wherever she is, she can still be seduced. These days, with texting, snapchat and everything else, it's easier than ever to find ways to do some graft work and seduce a woman. Of course, you might not see any action until you see her in person, but that doesn't mean it's not worth the time and effort.

And that's another place where guys go wrong. Time. A lot of guys knock off seduction because they think it takes 'too much' time. This is simply ridiculous. They think that there must be some magic formula out there which will work for them and that if you spend too much time with one girl, you are losing out on the opportunity with others. But think about this. On how many occasions has this actually worked for you? How many times have you given up spending more time with one girl because you haven't seen results in the time you've spent with her, and moved on to another girl only to be unsuccessful again. Let me assure you this, your sex life will see much better days if you spend the time to seduce one woman than it will if you spend merely an hour trying to seduce lots of women. You need to invest the time to get her in to bed. Remember when we spoke about trust earlier? Yeah, well that's what I'm talking about now, too!

When you talk to a woman, remember that you are trying to sell yourself and give her reason enough to believe that you are worth her time, and her investments. She needs to be able to trust that you want *her* for a reason, and that she isn't just another number in your attempts to get laid. If you want practice, find a long mirror and talk to yourself. Yes, it might be cringe at first, but it will be worth it when you are rewarded with better, more frequent sex. You might begin to realise why you haven't succeeded so far in seducing women. Your facial expressions might be off, you might be stuttering or pausing. If you can't persuade yourself that you are worth having sex with, then it's no surprise seduction hasn't worked so far. It's an art, really.

But there are some things I want to talk to you about. There are a few things which really do need to be brought to your attention before you go ahead and try to seduce someone again.

Make her *feel* wanted, and wanted *more* than anyone else in the room. She wants to know that you want her and that you aren't going to be thinking about anyone else. She doesn't want to be a second-place prize. It's all about her and you need to remember this, always. Of course, what you want is important on one level. I mean, you wouldn't be trying to seduce a woman unless you wanted sex yourself. But beyond this, it really doesn't matter what you want because you already want sex, and you already want to have sex with this one woman. But you need to be convincing her why she wants to have sex with you. It's all about how you make her feel.

It's probably time to go back to the mirror if you really want to understand this point. Even the simplest facial expressions can either make her feel wanted, or make her feel like you don't really care. There's a very thin line between them, so make sure you have this down! You need to practice expressing yourself in a way which makes her feel special. Practice. Practice. Practice. This is the key, because you are almost certainly going to fail unless you get yourself comfortable and familiar with being 'that guy'. Keep in mind how you talk, what you say, and what you do. All of which are just as important as the other and should never be neglected.

However, one thing to remember here is that all women are different. I mean, yes, sometimes the same old tricks will work on more than one woman, but still, each woman should be seduced on an individual basis. Some might react to cheeky humour, and others might react to some dirty talk in the club. You need to figure out the woman first before you try seducing her. And finally, make sure you invest enough time into this one woman. We spoke about this earlier for a reason! If you want to make her feel special and worth the time, you need to spend the time. Simple.

FOREPLAY MASTERY: THE ART OF FOREPLAY

When you think about foreplay, what goes through your mind? Probably oral sex and fingering. And you'd be right, this is foreplay, but there is a lot more than this that almost every man neglects. Here, we're going to go through all sorts of ways that can enhance your foreplay. It's worth remembering that is takes around 20 minutes to get a woman to an intense orgasm, so it's best not to go straight in for sex! Foreplay is a great way to get the both of you aroused and can make her orgasm so much better at the end of it all! If you're worried that you won't last longer enough to get her there, one simple way of solving this is by focussing heavily on foreplay to begin with and then have sex. It's also great for raising the sexual tension until she's practically begging for you to be inside her. It's all about making her want you until she can't resist.

1. Set the mood

Remember a while back we were talking about a woman's need for trust and comfort. This comes in to play right now. If you want to commit to foreplay before sex, you need to make sure that she wants it too and the best way to do this, along with seduction, is to set the mood and the environment around you.

This all seems like such basic stuff which is why it is baffling that no one really bothers anymore! Dim the lights, put on some quiet music in the background to fill the gaps, make sure it isn't too hot. I'm sure you can probably handle this yourself so get to it. Just make sure she is comfortable where she is and ready for what's coming.

2. Keep it Clean!

Your personal hygiene is your responsibility. Now, I'm not your mother, but keep it clean! Shower before seeing a girl, cut your nails, do your hair and shave/ style your beard! Nothing is more off-putting to a woman than being smelly, dirty down-under and looking like you haven't bothered. Imagine if the tables were turned and you went down on a woman who smells down there and hasn't showered? If she never shaved or cleared the grime from her nails, how would you react? You might even have been there before and I'm sure that it can't have been a good experience for you. So, please take my advice here. Keep. It. Clean.

3. Tease Her

A woman has erogenous zones for a reason! Play with her breasts, tickle her feet and stroke her forearm. The breasts alone have lots of different zones which can arouse a woman so don't just dive straight in to suck on her nipple. You might find it best to begin by feeling around the outsides of the breasts and build up the sensitivity and only then move on to stimulating the nipple. Start with your hands and then move on to licking around and sucking it. Do things in order when it comes to things like this because you need to build the stimulation; it's much more exciting that way.

4. Kissing

Believe it or not, kissing counts! And it's hands down the number one foreplay tool. Kissing shows a woman that you care about her and provides her with comfort, but the lips are one of the most sensitive parts of our body for a reason! Hopefully you can consider yourself to be a great kisser because it's probably one of the first things a girl notices once things get going.

What also great is that kissing can be on so many different levels. You can do frequent little pecks, playful and fun, or you can go really passionate and romantic. Both are great depending on the situation. You need to make sure that you evaluate exactly what the goal at the time is and reflect this in your kissing – the speed, the intensity, whether you should bite a little or use a bit of tongue. If you want a general rule here, start slow and then increase the intensity when things get a big hotter like when you're actually having sex. All these things are key parts of the build up to sex. I mean, imagine sex without any kissing what-so-ever. Weird, right?

You don't only need to limit yourself to her lips either! You can kiss and nibble her ear, you can gently kiss her shoulder, or when you go on to giving oral sex, you can start with kissing at the bottom of her legs and make your way up the inside of her thighs. Kiss her clitoris instead of just licking – it's a whole other sensation!

5. Biting and Nibbling

I mentioned briefly about biting the lips and nibbling around the nipples. There's something about biting that is really sexy and really raises the tension! When someone is biting you, they have to trust that you are being playful and aren't going to hurt them and it's this which makes it exciting. It makes a firl nervous, but in a good way. Her hairs will stand on end and her sensitivity will sky rocket.

Try gently biting around the back of the ear because it's a very sensitive area. Gently breathe down the back of her neck whilst doing so. Nibble gently on her nipples or on her shoulders and she will want you more than ever. Just don't start with this, seduce her a little and get the ball rolling.

6. Getting a Little More Rough

This one might depend on the girl you're with because some women will simply hate it. But anyways, spanking. You can spank before sex, or during sex – it's an in-the-moment kind of thing.

Make sure that she wants to be spanked, she might even ask for it! But when you do, ensure that you actually spank her bum cheeks and not above or below because that can be painful in a bad way. Spanking can really get things going and is good when things are going a bit faster and harder. I'd recommend spanking when she's on top and riding hard.

7. Pulling Her Hair

This is another one for when things are getting a bit rougher and is great when the woman you're with wants to be dominated. She wants you to be forceful and take complete control. Submission is sexy here. Just be careful. Whenever you try to be rough in the bedroom you absolutely HAVE to make sure that she likes it that way. If this backfires it's going to blow the whole operation.

It might be worth trying it slowly i.e. gently grabbing a bit of her hair and using it to move her head. Build it up and get rougher so that you don't just go straight in and yank it. Respect her and she will let you do practically anything when the time comes. If she does let you go for it, grab as much hair as you comfortably can at the base of her skull to reduce the tension and make it hurt less. Hair grabbing is about showing dominance and control, not causing her pain. Keep this in mind.

8. Fingering

Fingering is probably one of the first sexual experience any guy has ever had, and yet, it's probably the one thing that most guys struggle to get right. There is so much power in the ability to finger a woman well. It's most people's go-to move before sex.

When it comes to fingering a girl well, like everything else we've spoken about, it requires a build-up – you can't just jam you fingers up there and expect her to enjoy it. You need to start slow. Begin by gently rubbing the area, not just the bean, but the whole area. The key word here is gentle. Only when you see her behaviour respond to what you're doing should you start getting a bit heavier and faster. She might even push you hand in closer or inside her. When the time comes to put your fingers inside her, do it slowly. Rub around the outside and spiral your way in. But timing really is everything here. You want to make sure she is wet, and I mean dripping wet. That's her body telling you that you've done a good job and she's ready for you. If you don't wait then you aren't going to make her feel good, you're actually going to hurt her which is a big turn off.

Once your hands have made their way inside, you still aren't done. For guys, it's easy to get please – you just go faster and harder, but women are different. You need to explore inside of her, and if you're lucky, find her G-spot.

The G-spot in on the upper wall of the vagina. Once you've got your finger inside her, and you only really need one and this point, point it up and pull back gently. You're trying to find a slightly rougher area that will cause her immense pleasure. But you might not even find it! So, make sure that you're still making her feel good – you don't want her to feel like she's being examined! You want her to feel good until you 'happen to stumble' upon the G-spot. Once you've found it, bump up the speed and intensity of your finger movements. She will begin to moan and move her hips when you're hitting it right. You should be able to induce a G-spot orgasm and make her come!

9. Oral Sex

When it comes to oral sex, it's best to think about orgasms. The orgasm is primarily a reaction to signals being sent to your mind. The orgasm itself occurs in the mind, which kind of comes as a shock to a lot of guys because they simply assume that, because it is their penis going in to the girl's vagina that causes an orgasm, it must be purely biological. But I can't stress enough the importance of the female psychology here. You need to understand and appreciate this fact in order to ever have real success when it comes to oral sex. It's all about sending the right signals.

You're probably going to hate me here when I say you need to be patient. Again. But you simply can't dive in with your tongue and get to work, unless this is mid-sex and things are already really hot. Otherwise, you need to be gentle. She'll get a much better sensation that way and you can build up to something more intense. Remember, it takes about 20 minutes for a woman to reach an intense orgasm so make the most of the time early on and really focus on the foreplay! Build up to great sex! Once you realise this, your sex life will change forever.

Here's a tip, and I did kind of mention this earlier. Don't just go down on her. Start by kissing your way down to her tummy and pull down her panties. Then, make your way kissing back up the inside of her legs and focus on her thighs. Breathe. There's something so gentle and mood enhancing when a girl feels your breath on her sensitive areas. Breathe your way closer to the clitoris and then give it a gentle kiss. Transition in to something a bit more intense. You want her to be ready for you to lick her out – she needs to prepare herself.

You want to start around the clit, don't dive straight for it. You want to treat that little bean like it's the most precious thing you've ever come across. Take care of it. Tease it. Make its pleasure your only focus and she will go crazy for you. And don't just use your tongue. This is such a common mistake for no reason at all. Move your mouth and miss it. Move up and down with your head and use your jaw to reach new places. You want to explore the area.

Finally, hands free isn't an option. I mean yes, this is oral sex, but you should keep your hands busy. Try holding on to hers while you lick her out to figure out her reactions and what she wants to do next. Hold her legs apart and pin her down. Take control. You could even finger her at the same time and try to find her G-spot. Stimulate her in other ways like playing with her bum and boobs. Just do something that enhances her experience – if you stimulate multiple places she's much more likely to enjoy the experience and orgasm.

Just remember, when you go down on a girl, you want to be gentle, build things up, and keep a variety. If you just do one thing all the time it's going to get boring where she gets used to the sensation. Think about when you get a blowjob. It's pretty boring if the girl doesn't mix things up with her tongue or with her hands. It still feels good, but a good blowjob is nothing compared to a great one. Just don't be afraid to get a little messy because you will, but that's a good thing!

If she gets a bit more comfortable with having oral sex with you i.e. you've done it a few times already, you might want to look in to oral sex positions. The one you probably go for is to have her laying on her back and you lick in between her legs, but that puts you in control. If maybe she wants to take charge, you should have her sit on top of your face. That way she controls the speed and intensity and controls her own experience. This is great because she's the one that really knows what she wants. Keep this in mind.

PENETRATION MASTERY: THE ART OF PENETRATION

We're finally here. We've now covered virtually everything you need to know to get a girl in to bed, and to get her ready for amazing sex. It's time to learn how to make her scream. This has been your end goal since the start so if you need to recap everything so far, go ahead, otherwise, let's get started.

You might be thinking, 'the art of penetration? Really? Surely there isn't much to it?'. But take my advice here from a woman's perspective! You are wrong. Penetration deserves its own chapter, and here's why.

If you really want to be good at sex, and I'm pretty sure you do since you've come this far, you need to get in the mindset that each and every act you perform sexually is as important as the last. Sex is an experience, not just something we do for the hell of it.

When it comes to penetration, you want to focus on her, just like most things we've gone over. But remind yourself that if she's having a good time, you'll be having a great time. The focus should be on her reaching orgasm and she MUST reach orgasm. You can reach it at any time, but you need to put the time in to getting her there, otherwise you're just going be the disappointment that almost delivered, but failed at the last hurdle. It sounds harsh, but it's what you need to know.

Now, on to actual penetration. You have the basics down – put it in, thrust and pull out once the job is done. But does that really sound like a guy who knows what he's doing? Probably not. Penetration can vary and can re-occur even during sex. For example, it can feel amazing to have a guy pull out his penis fully and then re-insert it. There are even sex positions designed for penetration and re-penetration so don't just take my word for it! You can vary the spend, the angles and even the sex positions to make penetration more pleasurable.

Firstly, there's the speed that you penetrate a girl and for this we're talking about during sex too. A guy will generally have 3 speeds when he has sex – gently when starting out and being passionate, rhythmic and steady, or hard, rough and fast when she's approaching orgasm. You should never just stick to one because this gets boring and you need to be continuously stimulating different areas of her vagina in different ways to make sure she's getting the most pleasure out of you. It's just like what we said earlier when we discussed oral sex – you need to mix it up.

And don't be like every other guy who can't get it out of their heads that going at it like there's no tomorrow won't always make her feel great. If she isn't ready for you to go hard and fast she is simply not going to enjoy it – it could even hurt her! And the moment she gets turned off during sex you know you've failed because it's very hard to come back from. Unless you're having a sexy quickie when you don't have much time, this won't work and you will undo all your hard work so far.

The best way to make sure you know what your doing is right is to listen to her body language. If you feel her moving faster and more vigorously then speed things up, but if she's moving gently and is calm then keep things slow. If she's having a good time she will show you and when she is ready for harder sex then it will be clear. She is going to react to everything you do so take my word for it and react to how she acts.

Moving on, we have angles. There are virtually endless sex positions which all provide a different angle for penetration. See the missionary 180, for example. This position is featured later on in this book if you want to look at it in more detail, but the basics are like this. The woman is laid on her back in the typical missionary position, but to get a new angle, the man is facedown with his head at her foot end and penetrates her from that angle, hence the '180'. Her then rotates his him rather than thrusting in and out. This is just one of so many examples of using angles to give her new sensations. You can change things up mid-sex to hit the different walls of her vagina and stimulate her in other ways. Doggie Style is another popular choice, or cowgirl. Even if you don't change the position, you can still change the angle in missionary. Move your hips in a way that makes your penis contact different parts of her. You can even pull her legs together or push them further apart. You can put a pillow under her back to raise her hips. We'll talk about these in more detail later, but your goal here is to stimulate her in different places so she can experience different sensations. However, you might find one thing in particular that she really does like and it won't make any sense to change right this second. If she starts moaning you might want to keep doing what you're doing, speed things up and repeat. As I said earlier, react to how she acts.

You might find a lot of success trying to tease her a bit too. Instead of just putting it in, rub it around the outside of her vagina. Stimulate her clitoris. You can really get her going when she wants you inside her and won't put it in. I know you want to, but you can get her really worked up here and when you finally do penetrate, she will have an immediate gasp of satisfaction. Trust me, it's worth it! And when you do penetrate, there's no rule that you have to go the whole way in. It can be quite fun to have it put in a little bit of the way and then unexpectedly have it fully inserted. The excitement alone can be enough to get her on her way to an orgasm. If she's begging you to put it in, you've done well.

ORGASM MASTERY: HOW TO MAKE HER COME

We're finally here – the crème de la crème. The orgasm. That point when you know you've accomplished what you came here to do. She's happy, you're certainly happy, everybody's happy.

We know by now that you must work to get a girl to orgasm, and I mean a genuine orgasm. The sad truth is that most women end up faking an orgasm to avoid the awkward tension when her man knows he hasn't got her there. But not anymore. You now finally understand that the female orgasm is about more than just the physical act and you now know pretty much all you're going to need to get to that wonderful place.

I want you to remember exactly that. The orgasm isn't purely physical; the emotional and psychological elements are still so, so important. It's possible for a person to orgasm without even being touched. It's hard, sure, but it is certainly possible. I just need to demonstrate to you the significance of the mind here. It's a key part to getting a woman to her ultimate climax. Think about tantric sex. Now, you might not know a lot about tantric sex, but the idea is that sex is considered as virtually spiritual in nature – it's linked to a higher state of being. So clearly sex is more than the mere physical act of stimulating the nerves.

It's important, then, to remember that sex, like I keep reminding you throughout this discussion, is about a lot more than the physical act. I'm sure you've hear the saying that sex is 10% physical and 90% in the mind. I know this might be a little hard to believe at first, but by now I expect that you understand this saying a lot more now. The best sex should be an expression of how you feel towards your partner. This doesn't mean that it needs to be super slow and passionate throughout – you can still show your girl how you feel by having fun.

Moving on, I mentioned earlier about how there are multiple ways to bring a girl to orgasm. There's the vaginal orgasm, there's the clitoral orgasm, or you can even bring a girl to orgasm through anal sex or without even touching her! But we'll get on to this later. Firstly, I want to talk about vaginal orgasms and clitoral orgasms. The quite sad reality is that a lot of women very rarely experience vaginal orgasms, but rather find that clitoral stimulation is the only way they ever have been able to reach climax. That's why a lot of guys, and you might be one of them, tend to focus greatly on stimulating a clitoral orgasm because it's generally a lot easier and a lot more reliable. I don't really blame you. None-the-less, it's important that you don't disregard other orgasms that a woman can come to and understand how and why a woman comes to such an orgasm.

Not all women reach orgasm in the same way and not all women will reach orgasm every time they have sex. Some women need direct clitoral stimulation to reach an orgasm, while others can have clitoral orgasms through direct clitoral stimulation and/or sexual intercourse. This means that before you start trying to get her to orgasm, you have to experiment to find out what turns her on. You need to understand what you need from your partner to help her reach an orgasm. After a few experiments, you should have a pretty good idea of how to get there.

If you find that she needs clitoral stimulation to reach orgasm, make sure you and your partner focus largely on foreplay. This will turn you on and get you ready for sex and is a great way to bond with your partner to increase your chances of reaching an orgasm. Use whatever feels best – physical, oral or even a vibrator can massively increase your chances of getting there before sex. During intercourse, you should try positions that allow easy access to the clitoris, like cowgirl or spooning.

If you need clitoral stimulation through intercourse, try altered missionary positions. Try starting off in missionary position, bring your legs together between your partners and have him shit his weight so that pressure is applied to the clitoris when he thrusts.

If you need G-spot stimulation, the G spot is located on the front wall of the vagina. You will need to find the right angles and positions that allow deep penetration. Try missionary or doggy style. Reverse cowgirl is also a great position which allows you to control penetration depth and the angle you need to stimulate the G-spot.

We all know that women can orgasm, obviously. But a lot of guys are confused when it comes to a woman coming. Girl's often will tell you 'I just came', and they probably did. But what confuses a lot of guys is that women can ejaculate just like you! Of course, they don't ejaculate sperm, but a clear and odourless liquid – just like guys ejaculate cum, girls ejaculate this fluid. It's normal! And it's great. For whatever reason, this seems to baffle a lot of people because it just doesn't make sense to them and think that it might just be some sort of myth that has been made in the spotlight of pornography, but it's very, very real. Now you know.

And what's great is that if you've brought a woman to ejaculation you know that you've done well. Female ejaculation is the highlight of the female orgasm and is one of the most pleasurable sensations a person can feel. It's on par with full body convulsions and eye-rolling orgasms.

The most common signals that will tell you is a girl is coming can be seen by the way she acts. She will likely start moving with less control, her eyes might drift upwards and she will moan uncontrollably. But a lot of this is easily faked – I'm sure you've read a lot about fake orgasms and how so many women pretend to come. It shouldn't be this way, but it is. Now it's up to you to make sure that your partner never feels the need to fake again because you're genuinely making her scream!

If you need validation that your girl has is coming, the only sure way you will know is if you make her squirt. It's one thing that simply can't be faked and if she does you can guarantee that she really is having an amazing time. If she doesn't, don't be too disheartened because it can take time to get to know exactly what each individual girl likes and some find it easier than others to get to the point where they can squirt. Just note that they are generally caused by a combination of clitoral stimulation and G-spot stimulation. Mix it up, find out what she likes, and be responsive like always.

I did mention earlier how it takes 20 minutes to get her there and you should start with foreplay. Although general guidelines, there is a reason why these are such good ones. If you want to make her have a squirting orgasm, you need to put in the time to really heat things up before you even have intercourse. When you're fingering her, curl your index finger up and find that G-spot! Rub it hard and intensely as she's getting heated up. If you're going down on her, try to slip a finger in and do the same to stimulate her G-spot and her clitoris. She will be extremely wet – you should be able to hear how wet she is, not just feel it.

If you're successful here then the chances are that she won't have anything to say – she will quite literally be speechless! When a woman experiences such a hard orgasm she physically won't be able to say anything! She will be so overwhelmed by the sensation that there is no need for words. If you accomplish this then well done, you've done what very few guys ever manage to accomplish because they simply don't know or understand how to. But you do.

Finally, we should talk about the most talked about difference between guys and girls. Guys come, great! Buuuuut, there are limitations. Once a guy has come then he is physically unable to come again – there is a short period, around 20-30 minutes, where it is genuinely impossible for a guy to get hard again. It's a whole other story for women. We are able to have multiple orgasms over and over again. Unlucky for you, but we are massively blessed when it comes to sex. But it's not all bad. If you give her multiple orgasms then she is definitely going to reward you in return so long as you can last long enough (don't worry, we're getting on to that later).

When it 'comes' to giving a girl multiple orgasms, it's generally easier to make her come the second time than it is to make her come the first time, so put a lot of work in to it! Make her orgasm one way, and then change things up to try and make her orgasm another way. If it doesn't work, go back to the first way and try again. If you accomplish this, then there's a pretty great chance that she won't want to have sex with anyone else because she has you! You are all she needs.

ORGASM MASTERY: HOW TO BOTH HAVE A BETTER ORGASM

This section has a fair bit to do with the last chapter 'How to Last Longer', so I'm not going to go in too deep here. But anyways, you've probably met or at least heard about women that always find it so hard to have a complete orgasm or even those who have never, ever orgasmed! This comes across as such sad news because it shouldn't have to be this way. We are a highly sexual species and the only species that have sex for pleasure – we literally go out of our way to experience the best physical and emotional sensation we can, so why do we often fall short of this goal?

Again, I need to point out that guys and girls are different. We can both have immense pleasure from having sex, but girls certainly, undoubtedly get the better deal because they have the ability to have multiple orgasms. As a man, you simply can't.

So how do you give a girl multiple orgasms? I went over this briefly in the last chapter, but you are going to want to switch between clitoral stimulation and the G-spot each time she comes. You're going to need to repeat this over and over again and you could literally give her orgasm after orgasm! If you put in the time to do this, she will be mind-blown by you and reward you back in return. The better the time she's having, the better the time you're going to have.

When it comes to you as a man, there's no need to fear! You can still have an AMAZING orgasm so long as you know how to get there. And when I say that, I literally mean an orgasm like you've never experienced before. So many guys are unaware about how great their orgasm can be. It is highly underrated for many reasons. We'll talk about this later!

The challenge you are going to face as a guy when it comes to having a great orgasm is coming too early on. If you've masturbated before, and I mean, c'mon, you have probably come so quickly that you're still hard at the end of it and generally unsatisfied. You've had good orgasms and you've certainly had ones that were nowhere near up to scratch! This is what I'm talking about. For some reason, guys seem to have it in their head that all their orgasms are equal, but they aren't! You are still so capable of having an insanely satisfying orgasm! All you need to do is learn how to last longer and stay harder (check out the later chapter in this book, we'll go through it all!).

ANAL SEX

So, we know that a great deal of the female orgasm comes from clitoral stimulation or vaginal stimulation. Where does anal sex come in to it? Sure, for guys it's different. Guys have prostates which produce a fuller orgasm sensation when their anal region is stimulated, but girls don't. Why does anal sex appeal to some women and how do they orgasm from it? Well, believe me, there's an answer! I just want to point out here that anal sex isn't for every girl and for some women it will never be an option. Make sure that she wants to have anal sex with you if you are ever going to try it. I'd recommend bringing it up playfully to see how she responds and go from there. Bringing up anal sex can be a kind of sensitive topic for some women and some even get quite offended when you ask, so tread carefully! If she is up for it, here's what you should know.

Sex is 10% physical and 90% in the mind. We've established this. So now we apply it. This explains perfectly why some women love anal sex and can have amazing orgasms from it! Sometimes anal sex brings out a girl's dirty fantasies which makes it very exciting for her. For a lot of women, it's the curiosity that gets her going. For others, the excitement comes from the whole idea that anal sex is forbidden and shouldn't be done. In a lot of cultures and religions anal sex is even banned – it was punishable by law in a lot of countries and still is today in some! But whether you agree with this or not, it doesn't really matter right now. Assumingly you're ok with the idea of it considering you've come this far.

If you are going to have anal sex with your partner, keep all this in mind. She isn't biologically equipped to have an orgasm this way, but it's very possible if you target her fantasies, curiosity and emotional stimulation. You might find it helps to stimulate other parts of her body too like playing with her clit, boobs and spanking.

It's not just about the act either! Just having anal sex out of the blue probably won't be all you imagine and hope it will be – you need to put in some graft work first. Again, you need to make sure there is trust between you and that she is comfortable with the idea. The best way to do this, in my experience, is to cater to her curiosity and nature. Try and appeal to her adventurous and naughty side. It might take a while, but she will hopefully come around to the idea. If she doesn't, don't force it. Like I said, a lot of women will never be interested in anal sex and if you persist to nag her then you are simply going to kill the vibes between you both! And you don't want that to happen.

You're going to want to have hygiene in mind too, by the way. As you can imagine, anal sex isn't the most hygienic thing you can do sexually. You need to understand this when it comes to anal sex, and you need to make sure she does too. Otherwise hygiene alone could put you both off anal sex for life! Or at least a long while.

This isn't going to be the nicest part to read, especially because it's not what you want to see when you're thinking about sex, but it needs to be done so keep with me! You want to make sure that she has evacuated her bowels a few hours before you try anal. She's never going to be completely clean on the inside, but it's a good place to start. You also want to make sure that her movement is firm and solid, not running too thin. This is usually all that most couples do when they have anal sex because it seems reasonable, but I would recommend going the extra mile to make sure she is clean. You can invest products designed to clean out faecal matter from the anus. Just make sure she uses it a little while after her bowel movement. Also, you will probably want to use a condom to be extra safe. There is always going to be some bacteria in the anus and the area is also prone to tearing so this can help! It can also help to avoid STDs too so my strong advice to you would be to use a condom! Don't try anal sex otherwise. Then, you should be good to go!

If she has come around to the idea, you have one goal. Make. It. Great. Sure, she might be open to the idea, but if she hates it then she's probably NEVER going to let you do it again. And I mean never.

You want to start by, as you can imagine, making sure she is turned on and hot. You might want to try role play or targeting her fantasies to make sure she really is emotionally ready for this experience. Make her feel naughty and curious.

I'm sure you know that lube is virtually a MUST if you want to have anal sex. It really is so much tighter than the vagina and you might not even be able to get it in if you don't have some good lube. It isn't expensive so make the effort. Remember, if she hates it then it will never happen again so be prepared when the time comes. Some people use butt plugs to make it more comfortable especially the first time. This kind of depends on what she is open to doing, but if she likes the idea then she should use one for a couple of hours before. I'm sure I don't need to warn you that anal sex is going to be painful for BOTH of you if you don't at least use lube.

So, your girl is as clean as a whistle and ready for anal. But please, don't ever assume that anal sex is the same as vaginal sex because it's not. You can't just do what you've done so far here because it's a different experience completely. If you're assuming it's anything like what you might have seen in pornos or other pornography, just take a step back and listen up. You have to take it slow, especially if it's the girl's first time having anal sex. Communicate with her – she is nervous! Especially when she can feel it just outside and touching her bum. Put a lot of lube up, down and around your penis, and also on her anus! This is important. You might find that you need to add more lube while you're putting it in or after you've started having sex – there is always more lube! You'll find that a lot of the lube gets pushed back down your shaft when you put it in so make a real effort to remember to lube her up too!

When you are penetrating her, start slowly. Let her know that your penis is there and you're about to start putting it in. Be responsive to how she acts. If she looks like she's in too much pain then slowdown of stop for a second. Ask her. Talk to her and keep up the communication. She might be expecting some pain, but there's a difference between that and avoidable, unnecessary pain. Just make sure she is enjoying the experience.

Once you are in, don't suddenly think, 'right I'm in now and the hard part is over so I can just go for it'. Wrong. Keep it slow for the first few minutes. It will take this time for her to get used to it inside her and for her to open up inside. Make sure that she is still engaged in the act and not just taking it. Keep things sexy and passionate. Grope her or kiss her – just let her know that you are there. You want this to be intimate and not just some hard sex. Remember you are exploring her fantasies, but you want her to be comfortable too!

SEX TOYS – SPICING THINGS UP

S ex toys are quite widely considered a taboo subject and for that reason people rarely even talk about them! They are usually hidden away so they can't be found by anyone except the person who put them there. I find it hard to understand this because sex toys really can be the instruments that take your sex life to a whole new level. You've got down seduction, you've got your girl in to bed and you know what you're doing, but why stop there? There really is a whole other world of sex out there when you introduce yourself to sex toys.

I should point out though that the whole 'sex toys are taboo' concept isn't entirely a bad thing. Just like what we spoke about when discussing anal sex, the fact that sex toys are commonly thought of as a forbidden and naughty activity kind of makes them even better! They can target the same fantasies that your partner already has and really make things hot and more exciting. In my opinion, if sex toys are out there, why would anyone limit themselves from them? It doesn't make sense – if you want a great sex life, they are a must!

Remember what we were saying earlier about mixing things up and providing different types if stimulation. Well, sex toys are practically designed to do exactly this – vibrators and dildos nowadays have extensions to stimulate the clitoris during penetration, for example.

There is one significant difference between having sex with your partner and using sex toys – they are purely physical! Sex toys literally are there for the physical satisfaction which is why they can be serious players when spicing things up. The focus up to now has been split between making an emotional connection with your partner and providing physical pleasure, but now it's time to really focus on making her physically feel amazing.

Sex toys are amazing. Period. They are able to give women sensations that are genuinely impossible to get otherwise, no matter how good a man might be in bed. And there is a huge variety of things you might want to introduce her to i.e. whips. Blindfolds, dildos, vibrators, handcuffs. There are so many out there and in so many varieties. To put it plain, sex toys expand the parameters of pleasure from sex – they make the impossible, possible.

I need to make one thing clear for you here, though. A lot of men avoid sex toys like the plague because they think that by introducing sex toys to the bedroom they are simply get replaced by them. I get it, I mean, what need would there be for a man if sex toys are so good? But it's not true. By using sex toys, you're not using them as a replacement for you, but you're using them as an *extension* of yourself – they are a part of her sexual experience with *you*. I know I said that sex toys are purely physical, but that doesn't mean your partner doesn't know that it's you that is making her feel that way, not just the toys. She will associate the pleasure with you, which is why you really shouldn't be afraid to introduce sex toys in to your relationship. You just need to make sure that, when you use them, you make it your experience too. Don't use them like you're reciting an instruction manual that came with them, engage in the sexual experience with your partner! Take her to a whole new world and join her there. Make it clear to her that she needs *you* to feel this good, not just the toys.

That's not to say that you can't use sex toys during sex either, by the way. You can use vibrators on her clit while you're having sex with her to really get her going. Whips, plugs, ties, they can all be used during sex to make her really scream! So long as she is comfortable with what you're doing, you're good to go.

Sex toys aren't just for girls either. When you hear 'sex toys', yes, you probably do think of dildos and vibrators. So do I. But there are sex toys for men which makes sex for you better too! And for her. Cock rings, if you don't know, are rings made from rubber which constricts around the shaft of your penis and your balls. It sounds a bit strange, but it comes with a few benefits. Cock rings can make you harder and bigger when you're having sex. By constricting tightly at the bottom of your penis, it's actually trapping blood tightly in there which is obviously going to make you harder – blood comes in, but can't leave so quick. This makes you harder and bigger which is great, right?

It can also help you last longer for similar reasons. By constricting on the urethra, it's going to stop you from coming as quickly because of the added pressure. You're probably familiar with the feeling when you can feel yourself coming close to ejaculation when masturbating, but holding it off so you can continue. This isn't so different.

Finally, it can actually make sex feel a lot better. By having all that extra blood and pressure in your penis you become more sensitive and everything that happens to your penis becomes more pleasurable, be it oral sex or intercourse. You can even get vibrating cock rings. It's similar to a vibrator, but it stimulates her clitoris with each thrust you give making way for really good clitoral stimulation while you are stimulating her G-spot intercourse. Some men like the vibration, too!

HOW TO LAST LONGER IN BED

L asting longer. The one thing that pretty much every guy that has ever lived wants to be able to do. I mean, who wouldn't want to have more sex for longer! It's amazing and generally speaking, the longer you can last the better chance you're going to have when it comes to making your girl orgasm, cum, squirt, and scream! I'm sure this is probably one of the reasons you've got this book and one of the reasons you have come so far!

A lot of guys struggle when it comes to lasting in bed because it just feels so good. It's nothing to be ashamed of. I'm sure a lot of your mates have probably had digs at one another about how long they can last - it's what lads do! But it isn't really anything to be ashamed of, it's just something you will always want to do better. If you've ever seen a porno, and don't pretend that you haven't, you have probably thought, 'how has he possibly lasted this long doing what he's doing'. But don't ever compare yourself or the sex you have to porn. Most of it is set up, fake and unrealistic. That's not to say that we can't learn from porn, because we can, but you shouldn't compare yourself to it.

Keeping it up can be difficult. It's physically impossible to be completely hard through an entire sexual encounter – sometimes it might go down a bit and then get hard again, or sometimes it might just go flaccid, or sometimes you might prematurely ejaculate. It can be embarrassing and generally a horrible experience. I'm going to show you how you can change this! I'm going to teach you about how you can stay harder for longer, and last longer before you eventually orgasm!

Firstly, I want to talk to you about porn. I know you are going to hate me for sating this, but porn is bad. Not only does it give people unrealistic expectation of sex, but it can really influence your perception of sex. Some guys have watched so much porn so frequently that they have literally desensitised themselves to real life stimulation. They find is hard, or even impossible, to get erect when a naked girl is lying with them because the only thing that will turn them on is a fake video they found on the internet. Do NOT fall in to the trap. A lot of you will think that this won't happen to you, but it will eventually, and your sex life will be ruined. It's not worth it.

So, what is so bad about porn. Well, by watching porn, you are giving yourself an immediate pleasure response for doing absolutely nothing. You won't be ready for real sex when it comes to it. There's also very real differences between stimulation from watching porn and sex in real life. By watching porn, you are essentially conditioning your mind to be aroused by firm, hard and rapid movements up and down your penis when you masturbate. This is not the sensation you get when you have sex and people get to the point where other stimulation simply doesn't get them going. Not only are you going to ruin your partner's experience when having sex, you're going to ruin your own.

However, masturbation itself isn't necessarily bad for you. In fact, there have been many studies which praise masturbation by men and women. It's healthy and natural to masturbate, but just tone it down and don't do it too frequently, and DON'T watch porn when you do it. There really is no need. The only reason why you think you need to watch porn is that, probably from a young age, you have conditioned your mind that you NEED porn to masturbate and ejaculate. This is really bad for you and will often lead to a porn addiction. You will also begin to learn how to control your sensations and condition yourself to actually last longer. You can hold off your orgasms when you feel them coming and keep on going. You'll find that your orgasms get much better too! Ever had it where you've watched porn, masturbated and ejaculated, but you were still kind of hard and didn't come as much as you should have? Probably. That shouldn't happen and is more than likely the result of watching porn. You should always be aiming for a full and intense orgasm, not just getting the job done.

Practice is also one of the best safe, natural and healthy ways to last longer. It won't be a surprise to you that for most people, the more they have sex the longer they can last. Once you get used to the sensations then you are better able to control yourself and last long. So, have frequent sex! Of course, this is limited. It's not like you can have so much sex that you will last for 3 hours each time, but it will certainly help get you started.

Next, Kegel exercises. You might not really know what this term means and that's fine. Kegel exercise is when you activate the muscles in your groin. It really is no different than holding in urine for a long time or controlling it! You know how you can kind of control when you urinate or stop it halfway through, only to start again shortly after? That right there is you exercising everything you need to help control an orgasm. This comes in very handy when you know your partner is approaching orgasm, but you're already there. You can use this to help hold it off for a short while until she comes. Then you can practically ejaculate immediately when she does, and you can come together – something which couples often find hard to do. I mentioned earlier about learning from porn, well, this is a method that a lot of male porn starts do to come on the spot for the famous 'money shot' (you know what I'm talking about!). This might take some time and practice, but you will get there in the end. If you masturbate frequently you might want to try doing this to see how well you can control your orgasm. You'll find that you can masturbate for a lot longer if you get used to this technique and implement it. Then, when you do have sex, you'll know exactly what to do.

There are also other great benefits to this too! Once you master your Kegel control you will be able to have firmer erections of longer and make it hard again whenever it starts to go soft. When you clench these muscles, you're essentially pumping blood in to your penis on demand. Most guys don't know they have this ability. If you don't already know, an erection is the result of an increased blood flow to the penis so by pumping more blood in to the penis you're naturally going to make it harder.

Finally, performance enhancers do exist. A lot of porn stars take them to make them squirt more (if they're a woman) or make them last longer if they're a man. Viagra is probably the most common and popular enhancer for men which makes you stay hard for hours. There are also others which are designed specifically to help prevent premature ejaculation. Essentially, these supplements dilate your blood vessels in your penis so that you can maintain a sufficient amount of blood down there. But before you go out and buy anything like this, talk to your doctor. Make sure that they are safe to use for you personally and take in to consideration any side effects that may occur! I can't stress this enough. Talk to your doctor. They are very professional and friendly so never be ashamed to go to them about anything.

AFTER SEX: WHAT TO DO, AND WHAT NOT TO DO

Just because you've just had sex, you can't sit back and relax quite yet! I mean, you could, but you shouldn't. Your partner will notice what you do immediately after you've had sex and she won't be all that impressed if you just go to sleep! It's what most guys do and it's what most girls hate! Trust me here. She will be so appreciative if you comfort her after sex. Remember, you want her to keep coming back to you for more so me attentive to her needs – it's all about trust and comfort.

Firstly, you might need to clean up. If you've came and it's all over her bum or anywhere else, get a wet wipe and clean it off. This depends on who it is and how comfortable they are with you, but if she doesn't hint at you to do this, let her know where the bathroom is or somewhere else she can go to freshen up. She will need it! After sex, there is always going to be a lot of sweat and moisture on the bed. Once she has made her way to the bathroom, you have a perfect opportunity to freshen up yourself. Wipe your face down and make the bed a bit more welcoming for when she gets back.

You're also going to want to stay awake when she gets back, even if you want to go to sleep! It's normal to want to pass out but make the effort to not. After sex is one of the BEST times to talk to your partner because people feel very open at this point. It's the best time to bond with her and make her trust you. Then she'll want you back once you're gone. Try to stay awake at least until she passes out herself!

I just mentioned how it's good to bond with your partner after sex, but how do you do that? Well, this is pretty simple. Talk, giggle, cuddle, kiss. Make her feel loved, appreciated and happy that she has just spent her time having sex with you. After sex is the golden opportunity for you to become so much closer with your partner on an emotional level so don't let this go to waste!

Like I said, DO things to make her feel comfortable and special. DON'T just lie there and make no connection with her. You will only make her feel uncomfortable and unwanted. Things might become awkward and horrible for her and for you too. This isn't what you want her to remember about having sex with you! You want her to remember the whole experience as something great! The last thing she remembers should be positive, not boring and stale after all the work you've done. This is so much more important than most people realise. I promise you, make the effort here and you really will stand out from the crowd.

For the most part, anything you talk about here will be natural and fluid. After you have sex you become so much closer to that person and there shouldn't be any problems when it comes to conversation. It doesn't need to be a flat-out discussion, but a little chat and a giggle is a great way to finish things off.

14 DAY GUIDE TO A BETTER SEX LIFE

Romance can be a gentle topic in any relationship. Whether you've been dating for 6 months or married for 6 years affection in the bedroom can wane over time. Sometimes you might find it comes back naturally, but other time you might find that you need to give it a little bit of a push.

That's where this book comes in. Maybe you'd like to rediscover that strong connection with your partner, maybe you want to enlighten your sexual self-awareness and feeling more comfortable in the bedroom, or maybe you just want to have some more fun.

This 14-step guide to rejuvenating your sex life is a highly praised and effective way to get things back on track. It is perfectly normal for occasional 'dry' periods in a relationship with stress, children, work or other issues that arise in life all taking the attention away from the bedroom, but within 14 days, you have the chance to rekindle your love life in a way that feels comfortable, natural and effective, without feeling pressured whatsoever.

DAY 1

Take some time to talk with your partner.

Sex is about communication. If you want to make a positive change in your sex life you need to feel comfortable talking to your partner about it, and you'll both be grateful for it. Tonight, take 15 minutes to sit down with your partner to discuss the plan and make it work for you! Everybody's different and sometimes a compromise might be the best way forward to jumpstart what each of you want to get out of the experience. Maybe you could go for a brief walk or have a quiet chat before turning off the lights, whatever feels more comfortable.

Continue to make time to talk each night. Having a daily check-in with your partner is without doubt the best way to make sure you're both happy with where things are going and that you're comfortable – make time for each-other's needs. As well as helping keep things going, you'll feel more and more connected on a personal level each and every time you have the chat which will naturally bring you closer together.

Make your own goals.

Ultimately, by the end of the next 2 weeks you want your sex life to be better, but that doesn't mean that you can't take much more away! Improving your sex life involves your mind, your body and the relationship. You want to become closer to your partner, you want to feel sexier, you want to know that's how your partner feels too. Find the courage to ask your partner how they feel about the plan; what do they want to get out of it? Make a sexy goal to achieve – take your sex life to the next level. Approach sex with a positive attitude and mindset and see the results for yourself.

Ask yourself, what do I love about my body?

A lot of confidence in the bedroom comes down to self-esteem – how you genuinely feel about yourself: body and mind. What makes you feel beautiful? The truth is, body embarrassment should have no place in the bedroom and your sex life. When it comes down to it, you should love yourself and your partner will love you no matter how you feel about your body. Learn to love who you are and what you look like. Write down 5 things about yourself that you like, 5 reasons why your partner is attracted to you. Work on having a positive view of yourself. Build your self-esteem because there is no reason why you shouldn't feel confident in bed.

DAY 2

Have a long morning with your partner.

Stay in bed this morning. Turn off your 8.30am alarm and take some time to just stare in to each-other's eyes, smile, cuddle. Talking isn't the only way to communicate with your partner, so make the most of every moment you have to show each-other how you feel.

Say goodbye. Properly.

For most people, a simply 'goodbye' or a peck on the cheek has become normal before heading off to work in the morning or going out for the evening – it has become routine like brushing your teeth or brewing a morning coffee, but it really shouldn't be. Goodbye is a time to show your partner how you feel and make them remember you for the rest of the day. Take time to say goodbye before you or your partner leave for the day. Have a long, passionate kiss. Implement passion throughout your day and get passion back.

Dress sexy.

You don't need to wear sexy, expensive lingerie to be sexy, but try and make a little effort when around the home or getting ready for bed. Be subtle, but sexy. Instead of putting on the same old and baggy shirt that you've work to bed for the whole week, wear something that says, 'I think we're worth it'. It makes all the difference.

DAY 3

Morning sex.

Morning sex is important. Even if you're tired, even if you don't feel your best in the morning or you want to get to work early, morning sex makes sense. Cortisol levels are at the highest first thing in the morning. Then, after sex, you will release other hormones which will make you feel in a good mood for the rest of the day.

Make the bedroom a place for sleep and sex.

Your bedroom should be made for nothing else, but for sleep and sex. Get away from other distractions like TVs, phones and technology. Make your bedroom place that you look forward to going to. All it might take is some nice and new bedsheets and some new pillows. Make sure you make the bed every morning and get rid of clutter or mess. Keep your room tidy.

Talk dirty.

Sometimes, a bit of naughty talk can really be what you need to get the excitement back in to the bedroom. Even if you're not completely comfortable talking dirty, make it in to a joke. Have a laugh with your partner. Talk about your sexual wish list; talk about theirs. You don't want your sex life to become boring so keep things exciting! Introduce new positions. Introduce sex toys.

DAY 4

Have some alone time.

Ironically, rekindling a sexual connection with your partner might mean spending some time by yourself! Self-esteem is an important element to confidence in the bedroom and is an essential element to having great sex. You need to be comfortable with yourself, so spend time with yourself. Walk around the house naked, look at your body in the mirror when you're getting dressed, explore your body and rediscover what feels good. Caress yourself in the shower and in bed – learn more about yourself. There's nothing to ashamed of.

Sext.

Sexting is a popular way of keeping the fire lit in a relationship. Having an exciting conversation when your partner isn't around makes them think about you – it makes them want to be with you and your sex life will be rewarded when they finally are with you. You might even find you're more comfortable talking dirty over a text than in person!

Focus on foreplay.

Intercourse doesn't always need to be the end result of spending time under the sheets with your partner. Spend time on feeling good rather than just climaxing. Foreplay isn't dead. Use oil and a feather, be sensual. Massage and explore each other. You will feel much more connected after a session of sensual touching a few times a week instead of just having sex.

Exercise.

Healthy people have better sex. Period. Those who are physically active enjoy sex more and want to have sex more. Your self-esteem will skyrocket once you start an exercise regime, even if it is just 30 minutes a day. Your partner will be grateful for it too!

DAY 5

Pleasure yourself.

Some people think masturbation is 'taboo' or something that they should be ashamed of. Don't be. Masturbation is normal and much more common than people like to admit. Some sexual therapists will recommend masturbating for 10 minutes a day a few times a week. The 10 million nerves of the clitoris have the one function to make you feel good. Masturbation increases libido so make the time for it! Maybe you could experiment with a new vibrator or other sex toy, or maybe you won't need on at all. Whatever works for you.

Try yoga.

Yoga has become more and more popular in the mainstream market, and for good reason. Yoga can held increase your self-awareness, flexibility and circulation – all things that are good for a healthy sex life. Even if you're new to it, start slow and learn the basics. It might even turn into a hobby. You could even try and see if your partner wants to join in and try it with you.

Date night.

Date nights are brilliant. They help people reconnect, they relieve stress that built up over the week and increase attraction. A date doesn't need to be extremely expensive or extraordinary either, you just need to spend some quality time together. Put some thought in to the planning too. Maybe you spend the night going to the restaurant you went to on your first date? Or maybe you want to try something completely new? This can help make new bonds with your partner – new experiences release chemicals like dopamine and make you feel just like you did when you first started dating.

You might want to take turns planning date nights for each other – show each other how much you care. Talk about this one with your partner.

DAY 6

Hit the gym.

Taking a session at the gym can really boost your endorphins. It can also help with male arousal problems which are quite common. Inactive men are up to 60% more likely to experience erectile dysfunction so try and get your partner to come along with your and invest in an exercise routine. Research has also shown that couples feel more attracted to each other after exercising and sexual arousal increases. It also helps to relieve stress – a common reason why people don't feel like having sex or showing physical affection for their partners.

Plan check.

You've reached the middle of the plan now and it's time to check what you've done so far. Make sure you're keeping your bedroom an oasis for sex and clear of clutter. Make sure you're saying goodbye with a passionate kiss. Cuddle in the morning and keep having the chat each night. Keep to the plan.

DAY 7

Take a rest day.

Most people spend their days off doing chores or running errands for other people, but you need a day off! Turn off your phone and spend the whole day to yourself or with your partner. Lounge around and relax. Do nothing else.

DAY 8

Self-exploration: Talking to your partner.

Keep discovering your own body. People who frequently explore their own bodies have more satisfying and consistent orgasms. Tell your partner what you've learnt, and hear what they've learnt. This time make the chat a bit longer than usual. Sometimes great sex needs to be taught. Everybody's different and your partner needs to know what you like and what you don't.

Explore your fantasies.

Remember when you and your partner spoke about trying new things in the bedroom? Remember having some sexy talk? Well now's your chance to act on it. Bring up the conversation again on a more serious note. Get excited to try something new together.

DAY 9

Take a day away.

Taking a vacation can relieve all the stress in your life. Sometimes you just need an escape. And the best thing is it doesn't need to be anywhere exotic. Even taking a night away at a hotel can help couples feel like they're on a real vacation. And what's more? 'Vacation sex' is the ideal way to get that spark back to the relationship.

Act out the fantasy.

Tonight's the night. Live your fantasy. It doesn't always need to be something crazy and out there, but it can be if that's what you want. Perhaps you wanted to try roleplay? Take your chance now and see the results in the morning. Make sure you are the one that initiates the fantasy. It makes your partner much more comfortable this way and you will feel much more natural. Whether you're at home or spending the weekend away, make the most of your time today.

DAY 10

Have a laugh together.

After your chat tonight put on a funny movie or play a game that you both enjoy. Laughter is one of the best ways to connect with, and stay connected with, your partner. Laughter shows a genuine connection that can't be forced or made up – laughter is real in a relationship. Laughter is about connection. Sit together, make out, hold hands. Be together.

Show your partner some appreciation.

A compliment can go a long way in a relationship. Even the tiniest comments can make someone smile and relieve the stress that's built up. You might want to remind them that you're grateful that they are going through the plan with you. Remember, it might not be the easiest thing for them to be comfortable with! Show them affection and they will show it back.

Treat yourself.

You've done well this past week. Sticking to a plan like this can be quite demanding to begin with, so reward yourself! Buy yourself something sexy for tomorrow's date. Get some new lingerie or some makeup, whatever makes you feel better about yourself.

DAY 11

Date night.

Time for another date. Remember, if you planned the date last time, let your partner plan it this time. It's not a competition but try and be thoughtful towards one-another. And remember, date nights shouldn't stop happening at the end of the 14 days. Keep them going at least once a week and keep them fresh and exciting – they shouldn't be a chore! You should both look forward to spending the evening with each other. You could even save up to go somewhere a bit nicer once in a while.

Plan check.

You're getting towards the end of the 14-day plan now and it's time for another plan check. Go back over everything you've achieved with your partner tonight and make sure you're still giving it all the effort you can. The long-term effects will be worth it!

DAY 12

Have a massage.

Physical contact stimulates the release of oxytocin – the more that's released, the more desire a woman will have. It may cost a little to get done, but once in a while you will reap the rewards.

Back to foreplay.

Don't forget about taking a night off from sex and focus on fore-play. For a lot of people foreplay is more pleasurable than sex altogether and feel closer after having it. And it's not all about receiving! 70% of men say that they enjoy giving oral sex to their partners, not just receiving it! So, make an effort to do it. The goal doesn't always need to be intercourse.

DAY 13

Another day, another rest.

Time to take one final rest day to reflect on everything that
has happened over the past 2 weeks. Do whatever you feel like
doing whether on the list or not, with or without your partner.
Today is about you and you need to make the most of it. After
all, tomorrow is the end of the 14-day plan to get your sex life
back to how it should be.

DAY 14

Have a quickie.

Sex doesn't have to be planned or scheduled. Sometimes it's better to be spontaneous, no matter when it is or where you are. Keep things exciting. Have sex in the morning, afternoon or evening. It doesn't have to take a lot of time and you don't even need to reach orgasm! It's healthy in a relationship to spontaneously show affection for each other and will end the programme with a smooth transition back in to your day-to-day relationship. Of course, you can repeat the plan if you found it enjoyable, or simply realise now how much your sex life has improved whether you keep following the plan or not!

101 SEX POSITIONS

MAN TRAP

This is a variation of the missionary position. The female should lie back on a bed in the missionary position and have the male lay on top. As he begins to thrust, the female can wrap her legs around him and have more control over the speed and pace of sex.

This is great if you just want some simple sex. You can put little twists on the move like arching the back for better stimulation. Wrapping the legs around the male will also get him going a lot faster!

1. The female should lie on her back in the missionary position – legs open wide and slightly bent.

2. The male should position himself over the female and face her.

3. The male can then penetrate the vagina, just as in the ordinary missionary position.

4. As the male begins thrusting, or when it feels best, the female can wrap her legs around the male and 'trap' him, forcing him closer of allowing some extra room for him to re-position.

5. Tip: Using a pillow under the female's back can help

cause an arch. This will greatly increase pleasure and will make things much more comfortable when wrapping her legs around the male.

Safety Tips

This position can cause a lot of strain on the female's lower back, so make sure support is provided by using a pillow or cushion! Be sure to ask whether your partner is comfortable and not in any pain at any point and don't be ashamed if you need to say something because *you* are uncomfortable!

THE DECKCHAIR

The male should sit on the bed with his legs stretched out and his hands behind him to support his own weight. He should lean back and bend his elbows slightly. The female should then lie back on a pillow facing him and put her feet up on to his shoulders. She can then move her hips forwards and back and begin having sex.

This is an amazing position for very deep penetration for G-spot stimulation.

1. The male should sit on a bed with his legs stretched out. He can use his hands behind him to support his weight.

2. He should then carefully lean back and bend his elbows slightly for further support and control.

3. The female should then position herself by the male's feet, facing him and laying back on a pillow for support.

4. Once in position, the female can begin moving herself closer towards the male until her feet are up on his shoulders.

5. Finally, she can move her hips towards his penis for insertion.

6. In this position, once penetrated, it is best for the female to be in control and thrust her hips back and forth to get the best control and stimulation.

Safety Tips

This position can cause a lot of strain on the female's lower back, so make sure support is provided by using a pillow or cushion! Be sure to ask whether your partner is comfortable and not in any pain at any point and don't be ashamed if you need to say something because *you* are uncomfortable!

CORRIDOR COSY

This one can be tricky as you need to be in an enclosed area. The male needs to lean against a wall and needs to shuffle his way towards the floor until his feet are touching an opposing wall. The female should climb down on top of his legs, supporting her own weight. Her legs should be left dangling and she can begin thrusting.

This is a great one for adventurous and exciting sex!

1. Find an enclosed area with secure structures such as a thin corridor, hallway, or other appropriate settings.

2. The male should lean against one side of the wall and lower himself carefully by extending his legs outwards to the opposing wall.

3. IMPORTANT: The male's feet should always remain on the floor and securely in place at the base of the opposing wall.

4. The female should position herself on top of him and face towards him.

5. The female can begin lowering herself towards the penis for penetration, using either the walls around her or the male's shoulders for support. The female's legs should be left dangling while she is on top.

6. Finally, she can begin thrusting back and forth.

7. Tip: If this position is too taxing on the strength of either the male or the female, consider having the male position himself in a lower position so that the female's legs can reach the floor. She can then use her legs to help support her own weight.

Safety Tips

The male needs to make sure that he can support his partner's weight and that he isn't going to slip and fall to the floor completely. Likewise, the female should support her own weight as best she can to avoid potential injury.

TWISTER STALEMATE

The female should begin by laying on her back with her legs apart. Her partner should kneel down on all fours in between her legs. The female should then lift herself up, wrapping her arms around his chest for support. She should then slowly bring up her legs so her feet are flat on the bed.

This is a great position for deep penetration and stimulating the G-spot!

1. The female should lie down on her back with her legs apart and slightly bent at the knee.

2. The male should then position himself in-between her legs, facing her and on all fours i.e. on his hands and feet.

3. The female should then wrap her arms up around the male's chest for support. This will require some strength from the female.

4. The female can then bend her legs and begin to raise her hips. Her feet should now be flat on the bed.

5. Finally, she can guide the penis into her vagina for penetration.

Safety Tips

This position requires some upper body strength from the female. She should make sure to be holding on tightly to her partner as he thrusts.

THE SPIDER

You should start by facing each other. The female should climb on to her partner's lap and allow penetration. Her legs should be bent on either side of him and the male should be doing the same. The female should lay back first, slowly followed by the male, until both heads are on the bed. Now, move slowly and calmly.

This is a great one for slow sex to enhance stimulation before trying to reach climax – a good one if you have a lot of time.

1. Both the male and female should begin by sitting on a bed and facing towards each other.

2. The female should then shuffle forward and sit on her partner's lap.

3. This is the point where penetration should occur. The female must remain on top of her partner's lap.

4. Once penetrated, the female should slowly lean backwards and bend her back until her head is on the bed. Her arms can then be positioned outwards until comfortable.

5. The male should repeat this stage, leaning back slowly until his head is on the bed.

6. The female can then begin thrusting forwards and backwards.

Safety Tips

This position requires penile flexibility, else there is a risk of the male straining his suspensory ligaments!

If you want to find out if the male's penis is flexible enough, have him stand against a wall. Pull his penis gradually down. If the penis is able to point directly down to the ground without causing pain then you should be fine to perform this position, but still be careful.

The female should stay still when the male is initially penetrating her and guide the penis to the vagina. The female should wait while he finds the most comfortable position and angle to thrust without injury.

SPEED BUMP

The female should lay on her stomach and spread her legs. The male should then enter from behind.

The benefit of this position is that things can heat up and speed up very quickly. It is a great position for getting a little rough or if you're having a quickie!

1. The female should lay down on her stomach and spread her legs as wide as she can whilst remaining comfortable.

2. The male should position himself on top of the female with the aim of penetrating from behind, both facing the same way.

3. Once in the position, the male should use his arms to support his weight while he guides his penis towards her vagina for penetration.

4. Finally, the male can perform upwards and downwards thrusts.

Safety Tips

This position can cause a lot of strain on the female's lower back, so make sure support is provided by using a pillow or cushion! Be sure to ask whether your partner is comfortable and not in any pain at any point and don't be ashamed if you need to say something because *you* are uncomfortable!

TRIUMPH ARCH

T he male should sit down with his legs stretched out straight. The female should straddle him with her legs either side and kneel down over his penis. Once she has been penetrated, she can lean back until laying down on his legs.

This position can give the female a great orgasm and the male is able to stimulate her clitoris during sex.

1. The male should sit down on a bed with his legs stretched out and straight.

2. The female should straddle over the male, bending her knees until over his penis.

3. Once in position and penetrated, the female can slowly lean back until she is laying down on his legs.

Safety Tips

This position requires penile flexibility, else there is a risk of the male straining his suspensory ligaments!

If you want to find out if the male's penis is flexible enough, have him stand against a wall. Pull his penis gradually down. If the penis is able to point directly down to the ground without causing pain then you should be fine to perform this position, but still be careful.

The female should stay still when the male is initially penetrating her and guide the penis to the vagina. The female should wait while he finds the most comfortable position and angle to thrust without injury.

THE STANDING WHEELBARROW

For this position, begin in the doggy style position and have the female rest her forearms on some pillows. Her partner should kneel down behind her with one knee bent up to keep himself steady. Once he has penetrated, he should hold her legs and slowly lift her up as he stands.

This position is great if you are just experimenting and just having fun! Otherwise, it is a bit difficult and isn't very well rated for sensation.

1. The female should begin on her hand and knees, facing away from the male (the doggy style position).

2. The female can lean her upper body down towards the floor and rest her forearms on a pillow.

3. The male should kneel down behind her with one knee bent for extra support.

4. He can then position himself towards her for penetration from behind.

5. Finally, the male should grab hold of the female's legs, wherever comfortable and secure, and support her weight as he carefully raises to a standing position.

6. He can then thrust forward and back.

Safety Tips

The male should keep his knees slightly bent when thrusting. If either of you feels uncomfortable during the position, then you should let the other know and try something else! This one isn't for you.

SULTRY SADDLE

In this position, the male lays down on his back with his legs bent and apart – the standard position when the male is on the bottom. The female should slide herself between his legs, almost at a right angle to his body. For support, one hand should be placed on his chest, the other on his leg.

This position relies on the female rocking back and forth until she can feel him hitting her G-spot. The great thing about this position is that the female is completely in control so is one of the better one if G-spot stimulation is what you need to reach an orgasm.

1. The male should lie down on a bed on his back, facing upwards. His legs should be bent at the knee and apart.

2. The female should position herself over the male on her feet or knees, whichever is most comfortable.

3. She can then lower herself to allow for penetration.

4. Once penetrated, the female should place one hand on the male's leg, and the other on his chest for support. She can then use these supports to help her thrust and control her stimulation.

Safety Tips

This position can cause a lot of strain on the female's lower back, so make sure support is provided by using a pillow or cushion! Be sure to ask whether your partner is comfortable and not in any pain at any point and don't be ashamed if you need to say something because *you* are uncomfortable!

THE PROPELLER

The female should lay on her back with her legs straight and together. The male should lie down on top but be facing down towards her feet. Once penetrated, the male should make small motions with his hips instead of thrusting.

This is a very difficult position and takes some practice to master!

1. The female should lie on her back with her legs straight and together.

2. The male should position himself on top of her in the 180-missionary position i.e. over the female but be facing her feet. He should, as usual, be using his arms for support to hold his body weight.

3. The male can then shuffle backwards until he is able to penetrate the female.

4. Once penetrated, rather than thrusting back and forth, the male should rotate his hips in small circular motions in a 'propeller'-like movement.

Safety Tips

This position requires penile flexibility, else there is a risk of the male straining his suspensory ligaments!

If you want to find out if the male's penis is flexible enough, have him stand against a wall. Pull his penis gradually down. If the penis is able to point directly down to the ground without causing pain then you should be fine to perform this position, but still be careful.

The female should stay still when the male is initially penetrating her and guide the penis to the vagina. The female should wait while he finds the most comfortable position and angle to thrust without injury.

THE LUSTFUL LEG

S tart by standing close and facing each other. The female should have one leg on the bed and the other on top of the male's shoulder, whilst wrapping her arms around his back and neck for support. Then he should carefully penetrate.

Once in position, this is a great move that feels fantastic! It does, however, require some endurance.

1. Both the male and female should begin by standing up beside a bed and facing one another.

2. The female should wrap her arms around the male's neck and shoulders for support.

3. The female can then raise one leg on to the edge of the bed. The other leg can then be raised up to the male's shoulder.

4. Once in position, penetration can take place.

Safety Tips

This position requires penile flexibility to avoid the risk of the male straining his suspensory ligaments!

If you want to find out if the male's penis is flexible enough, have him stand against a wall. Pull his penis gradually down. If the penis is able to point directly down to the ground without causing pain then you should be fine to perform this position, but still be careful.

The female should stay still when the male is initially penetrating her and guide the penis to the vagina. The female should wait while he finds the most comfortable position and angle to thrust without injury.

THE WATERFALL

The male should sit in a sturdy chair. The female can then climb on top with her legs either side of him. She should lean back until her head is on the floor.

The clitoris is very accessible in this position so is great for stimulation during sex. There is also a lot of friction inside the vagina so this is a great all-rounder for reaching orgasm.

1. The male should find a secure chair and sit on it.

2. The female can then position herself facing towards the male with her legs either side of him.

3. The female should then lower herself on to his penis for penetration.

4. Once inserted, the male should use his hands to support the female behind her back and bottom.

5. The female should then slowly lean backwards until her head is on the floor.

6. Whilst performing step 5 above, the male should take care to support the female's weight however necessary, and the female should take care to move slowly to ensure that the male is not experiencing any strain or discomfort.

Safety Tips

This position requires penile flexibility, else there is a risk of the male straining his suspensory ligaments!

If you want to find out if the male's penis is flexible enough, have him stand against a wall. Pull his penis gradually down. If the penis is able to point directly down to the ground without causing pain then you should be fine to perform this position, but still be careful.

The female should stay still when the male is initially penetrating her and guide the penis to the vagina. The female should wait while he finds the most comfortable position and angle to thrust without injury.

A pillow should also be used on the floor to support and give comfort to the female's head during sex.

THE CHALLENGE

This is a difficult position (hence the name) and shouldn't be attempted unless you are confident and have tried lots of different positions before – it requires strength and flexibility.

The female should stand on a chair and bend her knees until in the sitting position. She should lean forward with her elbows on her knees. The male should then enter her from behind.

This one is hard to master. If it is too hard for you, you could also have the female simply stand on the ground and lean forward on to a chair as shown in the illustration below.

1. A sturdy and secure chair should be found for this position. It may be useful for the chair to be against a wall.

2. The female should mount the chair and stand up, facing towards the back of the chair and away from the male.

3. She should then carefully bend her knees until in a sitting position.

4. The female should then place her elbows on her

knees, and hold on to the back of the chair with her hands for support.

5. Finally, once comfortably in position, the male should approach the female from behind for penetration.

Safety Tips

Make sure the chair is very sturdy and you have good footing. The male should support the female throughout and should have a firm hold of the female's waist to keep her steady.

THE SUPERNOVA

For this position, the female should begin on top of the male on a bed or other comfortable place. The male should have his head near the edge. The female should place her feet either side of him and allow penetration by squatting down on his penis. She can then lean back on to her arms behind her.

The female should rock back and forth until she can feel herself reaching climax. When reaching climax, she should lean forward on to her knees and shift the male's upper body off the edge of the bed until she reaches orgasm.

This position is all about timing, but if done right can be really fun and give a great orgasm.

1. The male should begin by lying down, facing upwards and with his knees slightly bent and apart. His head should be near the edge of the bed.

2. The female should place her feet either side of the male's waist and squat down in a straddle position for penetration to take place.

3. The female should then place her hands and arms behind her on the bed and lean backwards. Her arms should be locked and providing most of the support.

4. She can then begin thrusting back and forth.

5. When approaching orgasm, the female should launch her upper body forward and on to her knees. This should slightly shuffle the male's head and upper body off of the bed.

6. Tip: Ensure that the timing is right with the once – it might take some practice. But, once done correctly, this can lead to a fantastic orgasm.

PIRATE'S BOUNTY

This position is great when you and your partner want to go a bit more out there to reach orgasm. It allows for deep penetration and total clitoral stimulation so is amazingly efficient at getting you to an orgasm.

To get in this position, the female should lay down on her back and the male should kneel in front of her. She should place one leg on her partner's shoulder and the other around his thigh. A pillow can also be used under the female's back to provide support.

1. The female should lie on her back facing upwards towards the ceiling with her legs apart.

2. The male should kneel in front of her, facing towards her.

3. The female should place one leg up on the male's shoulder (whichever is most comfortable) and the other leg should remain beside his thigh.

4. A pillow should be placed under the female's back to provide support and place her in an arch to increase stimulation.

5. The male should then penetrate the female.

6. Whilst having sex, either the male of the female can

easily stimulate the clitoris for further stimulation. This is best done when the female is approaching orgasm.

ADVANCED DOGGY STYLE

This is a simple variation of the traditional doggy style, but with a much better chance of achieving an orgasm.

To do this, assume the normal doggy style position and guide the female's head until it is against the bed. Her back should be bent slightly with her bum in the air. Now, place a pillow or blanket under her stomach to rest on. Make sure the female is relaxed. Thrust downwards at a hard and steady pace for several minutes until she reaches orgasm.

1. The normal doggy style position should be assumed by both the male and the female - the female should be on her hands and knees, facing away from the male.

2. The female should allow for a slight inwards arch in her back i.e. she should raise her bottom and chest whilst allowing her stomach to arch inwards towards the bed.

3. A pillow or large blanket should be placed under the female's stomach for her to rest on and she can then lower her upper body closer to the surface of the bed.

4. Finally, the male can penetrate from behind.

5. The male should continuous thrust in a firm downwards motion at a steady pace of several minutes.
His motion should become faster and harder as the
female approaches orgasm.

G-SPOT MISSIONARY

Assume the normal missionary position. Then place the female's legs on to the male's shoulders. A pillow should be placed under her lower back for support and comfort. Slightly push forward until the female's bum lifts off the surface of the bed. Begin thrusting hard at a consistent pace. You can bring yourself closer to her to be more intimate or further away to thrust harder.

1. The female should lie down on her back, facing upwards with her knees slightly bent and legs apart. A pillow should be placed beneath the female's back to create an arch and provide support.

2. The male should position himself on top of the female, facing her and using his arms to support his body weight.

3. The male should penetrate the female just as he would in the ordinary missionary position.

4. Once inserted, the male should slightly push forward (before thrusting) in order to raise the female's bottom slightly off the surface of the bed. The female's bottom should remain elevated from the surface of the bed throughout.

5. Finally, the male can begin thrusting at a constant and firm pace.

6. Throughout this position, the male can slow down his thrust and bring himself closer to the female for intimacy, and lift away from the female for harder and faster thrusts as she approaches orgasm.

FLATIRON

The female should lie face down with her hips slightly elevated. A pillow should be used for support under her stomach. She should spread her legs out and straight. The male should mount her from behind with his legs on the outside of hers and penetrate. This position allows for easy access for anal sex or vaginal intercourse, but limits access to the clitoris so keep that in mind if you need clitoral stimulation.

1. The female should lie face down on a bed with her hips slightly elevated. Her legs should be comfortably apart.

2. A pillow should be placed under the female's stomach for support.

3. The female should now spread her legs further apart and keep them straight.

4. The male can then position himself on top of the female using his arms for support.

5. Once in position, the male can penetrate the female virginally or anally and begin thrusting. His legs should on the outside of the females, but they can remain on the inside if the male finds this uncomfortable.

6. The male is now in control and can build up to a hard thrust.

THE SUNDAY AFTERNOON

This is a much easier position to try when you want to reach an orgasm. It's a great choice for easy access to the clitoris if you need clitoral stimulation to reach climax. It is a variation of an X position, like The Scissors.

The male begins laying on his side and the female on her back. She puts one leg over his outer-side hip and the other wrapped around his lower leg to pull him close in. The male gently penetrates and begins thrusting upwards.

1. The male should lay down on his side beside the female. The female should begin by lying on her back.

2. The female should then place her outside leg over the outer-hip of the male. The other leg should then wrap around the male's lower leg. At the end of this movement, the female should have transitioned from being on her back to being on her side, facing the male.

3. The female can then use her legs to bring the male in close and allow for penetration.

4. The male can then gently begin thrusting towards

the female in an upwards motion.

MASTERY

This is a version of the cowgirl position and doesn't ask for too much physical effort from either partner, but give the male easy access to the clitoris and the breasts for stimulation during intercourse.

The male and female should face each other in the cowgirl position, with the female seated on his lap. Her legs should be kneeling outside his. The position allows for couples to get close during sex and lean back for new sensations.

1. The male and female should assume the cowgirl position. This is achieved by the male lying on his back with his knees slightly bent and his legs slightly apart. The female can then straddle on top of the male's hips.

2. The female should transition so that she is in the same position, but resting on her knees rather than her feet.

3. The female should take control of allowing penetration by guiding the male's penis inside of her.

4. This position allows for a lot of variation depending on how the female is feeling during intercourse. She can lean forwards to come close to the male for intimacy, sit upwards for firmer thrusts or lean backwards using her arms for support when approaching

orgasm for G-Spot stimulation.

5. When leaning back, the male also has very easy access to provide clitoral stimulation.

SCISSORS

This is an X position and can be a challenge for those not willing to commit to it. The female should lay down on her back and her partner should enter her from the sides – her clitoris should be up against his top leg.

1. The female should lie down on her back, facing the ceiling.

2. The female should ensure that her legs are open wide to allow access by the male.

3. The male should begin in a sideways position away from the female with his feet in the same place as the female's.

4. The male can then begin moving towards the female between her legs.

5. As the male approaches, the female should raise her back and bottom to allow the male's lower leg to be positioned underneath.

6. As the male shuffles closer to the vagina, the female should help by positioning herself closer to allow for penetration – the female's clitoris should be up against the male's outer leg's thigh.

7. Penetration can now take place.

8. Once both the male and female are comfortable,

both can begin gently thrusting towards each other.

THE DIRTY DANGLE

B egin by having the female lay down on her back at the foot end of the bed. Have the male mount on top in the missionary position. The female should start moving back little by little until her head, shoulders and arms flay off the back of the bed towards the floor. The excitement of this position can be a new experience for lots of people and encourage orgasm.

1. The female should lie down on her back at the foot end of a bed.

2. The male should mount on top of the female in the missionary position, using his arms to support his weight.

3. Once in position, the female should start shuffling slowly backwards until her head, shoulders and arms flay off the back of the bed towards the floor.

4. Both the male and female should support each other during the above movement to ensure both are secure.

5. The male can then penetrate and begin thrusting.

6. The increased blood flow to the female's head aims to provide a greater and more fulfilling orgasm. This can be done before or during intercourse.

LAZY MALE

With this move, there is less thrusting involved and move up and down motions. There is lots of eye contact which can bring you closer to your partner and increase your chance of reaching an orgasm together.

For this position, the male should prop his body up with some pillows against a wall or the headboard of the bed. Here you can control the rhythm of sex. Have the female sit in the cowgirl position with her legs wrapped around his body and stay up and close.

1. The male should sit up against a wall or the headboard of a bed, using pillows for support.

2. The female should position herself above the male's hips and squat down to a straddle position.

3. The female can then transition into a kneeling straddle position and allow for penetration.

4. The female can then control the rhythm of intercourse as she begins thrusting up and down.

FACE OFF

Have the male sit down on the edge of the bed or sofa. The female should sit down on his lap, facing him. From here there should be a lot of friction on the clitoris which is great for reaching orgasm if you need direct clitoral stimulation to reach an orgasm.

1. The male should find a sturdy bed or sofa and sit towards the edge.

2. The female should position herself over him with her legs either side and lower herself down on to his lap facing him.

3. As the female lowers herself, she should reach a kneeling position with her legs either side of the male.

4. The female can then allow penetration by guiding the penis towards her vagina.

5. During this position, the female should thrust forwards to increase the friction on her clitoris and achieve the maximum stimulation possible.

THE OM

For this position, have the male sit down with his legs crossed while the female sits on his lap, facing him. Next, the female should wrap her legs around him and his legs should be wrapped around the back of her, still crossed. Pull each other close together and rock back and forth. You should look each other in the eyes as you climax.

1. The male should sit down, either on a bed or the floor, with his legs crossed.

2. The female should position herself over the male and be facing towards him.

3. The female should wrap her legs around the back of the male's bottom and cross them over behind him.

4. Penetration can now take place.

5. Once penetration has been achieved, both the male and female can pull each other close and rock and forth.

This is an intimate position and encourages both partners to remain close. The aim is to achieve good eye contact as the female approaches orgasm.

THE SEA SHELL

Have the female lay down on her back with her legs raised up and out. The male should lie on his stomach on top and be facing her as he penetrates, just like the missionary. The female's legs should be far apart to allow deeper penetration for G-Spot stimulation. It will also allow for some clitoral stimulation as he is on top.

1. The female should lie down on her back with her legs raised up and apart. She may use her arms flat on the bed to support her or hold on to both legs until the male is in position.

2. The male should lie down on his stomach and face her, much like the missionary position.

3. Using his arms to support his weight, the male should guide his penis towards the vagina for penetration.

4. The female should keep her legs wide apart during intercourse.

5. Once the male is in position, he can push forward to help keep the female's legs up in the air. She can then use her arms for support by placing them flat on the bed beside her.

SQUAT

This is a simple and commonly used position. The male should lay on his back on top of a bed. The female should straddle on top and lower herself slowly, guiding the penis into her vagina.

The female is again in control in this position and should raise herself up and down, using the bed or the male's chest to support herself.

There is a reason that this is one of the most used positions – it's great for sensation! And gives the female a good workout. The male also has quite easy access to the clitoris to help stimulation when reaching orgasm.

1. The male should lie on his back at the top end of a bed, legs only slightly apart and straight.

2. The female should position herself over his waist and lower herself in a squatting position.

3. Once in position, she should guide the penis inside of her.

4. Once inserted, the female can raise herself up and down at her decided pace.

5. The female should be squatting with her feet on the

bed in this position i.e. not on her knees.

ONE UP

This is an oral sex position. The female should lay on a bed with her rear close to the edge. She should raise one of her legs and hold it in position by wrapping it around her thigh. The male should kneel down between her legs and get down on her!

1. The female should lie down on a bed with her bottom very close to the edge.

2. The female should then raise one of her legs up into the air and wrap her foot around her other thigh.

3. The male can then kneel down on the floor facing towards her. The male should grab hold of the female's body and engage in oral sex.

4. During this position, the female is able to shift her bodyweight to dictate where the male stimulates her.

This is great foreplay before sex.

FACE TO FACE

In this position, you should sit opposite your partner and the female should slide herself on to the male's lap and sit on top of him. She should wrap her legs around his body until they are touching behind him. The male should then do the same and cradle her bum. Rock back and forth together and get close!

1. Both the male and female should sit opposite each other and face towards one another.

2. The male should cross his legs and allow the female to shift on top and sit on his lap.

3. The female should wrap her legs around the male until her feet are touching behind him. She can then allow for penetration.

4. Once inserted, the male should also wrap his legs around the female and cradle her bum with his hands.

5. Both the male and female should now rock back and forth for intimate and close intercourse.

This is a great one for getting intimate – it is a slow pace position and is great for stimulation building up to an orgasm. There is also a lot of clitoral stimulation during this one.

THE STAND-UP

The female should turn and face a wall several feet away with her bum slightly suck out. The wall should be used as support. The male should then gently insert his penis – he can bend his knees to lower himself if there is difficulty finding access!

1. The female should turn and face a wall several feet away from her.

2. The female should lean forwards and rest her forearms against the wall for support. Her bottom should be slightly tucked out.

3. The female may slightly bend her knees for additional comfort if necessary.

4. The male should approach the female from behind. He should grab hold of her waist and slowly penetrate. The male may also find that he needs to bend his knees slightly before penetrating if there is difficulty getting access from behind.

5. The male can then thrust back and forth. He may hold on to the waist of the female. He may also hold

on to her shoulders with his arms straight. If so, the female should slightly arch her back inwards.

The great thing about this is that the female can thrust backwards as the male is thrusting forwards so you can both control the speed of things!

HOBBY HORSE

This position requires a chair. Make sure it is reliable and strong.

The male should lay back down on the chair, keeping his body parallel to the ground. The female can then saddle up facing away from him and with her feet on his knees.

1. The male should lie with is back down across the body of a chair. He may use his arms to support him by placing his hand firmly on the floor. His feet should be firmly on the floor.

2. The female should then position herself with her legs either side of the male's waist (facing away from him) and squat to allow penetration.

3. The female should then lean back and rest her hands on either the male's chest area or on the edges of the chair itself.

4. Finally, the female should bend her knees and lift her legs so that her feet and resting on the male's knees.

5. The female can then thrust back and forth to engage

in intercourse.

6. Once the female is in position, instead of keeping his hands on the floor, the male may grasp hold of the female's waist/breasts for support and stimulation.

This move requires a lot of core strength from the male to hold the position but is a fun one where the female is in control.

THE ELEVATOR – PRACTICE MAKES PERFECT

This is an oral sex position so is great for foreplay.

The male should be standing and the female kneeling in front. This is a basic oral sex position. Be sure to mix up the speed during oral sex to make the experience better for the male.

1. The male should start by getting into a standing position.

2. The female should then kneel in front of him, facing him.

3. The female can then engage in oral sex.

4. The is a very versatile position and the female is free to alter the speed and sensations she provides the male during oral sex. She may also use her hands whilst doing so.

5. Alternatively, the male may thrust towards the mouth of the female while she holds her head steady. She may also benefit from the male using his hands to help hold her head in place.

The more you practice, the better you get!

CARPET BURN

In this position, the male should be kneeling down on a carpet, bringing one knee in front of him. The female should then kneel down in front of him and move to allow him to penetrate her. She should use his body for support and both can begin to thrust.

1. The male should kneel down on a carpet with one knee bent out in front of him.

2. The female should kneel down in front of the male, facing him. The female should also have one knee bent out in front of her but this must be the opposite knee to the male.

3. The female should then shuffle towards the male and slot herself between his knees; her bent knee outside of his knee on the floor, and her knee on the floor inside of his bent knee.

4. Once in position, she may allow penetration and both can thrust towards one another.

BEWARE OF CARPET BURN. The name says it all although that's where the excitement comes from!

THE LOTUS BLOSSOM

The male should go first, sitting with crossed legs. The female straddles on top and wraps her legs around him tightly. She can begin moving once he has penetrated, and he can help by raising her up and down.

1. The male should begin by sitting with his legs crossed.

2. The female should then sit on his lap and allow penetration while facing towards him.

3. The female should then very tightly wrap her legs around the male.

4. Once in position, the male should place his hands underneath the female's bottom and help raise her firmly up and down, pulling her towards him on the way back down.

In this position, the male has easy access to the female's upper body so is great for kissing and being intimate. Just make sure you are both comfortable before you begin!

BRIDGE

The male should lay across two sturdy objects with his body hanging between them. The female should sit on top of him from the side. She should then slowly bring one of her legs up and over so that she is now facing outwards to the side of her partner.

1. The male should lay across two study objects (such as two fixed countertops) and allow his body to hang between them. The male should face upwards towards the ceiling and may require pillows/ blankets for comfort on his shoulders and legs.

2. The female should mount on top of the male with her legs either side of his waist.

3. The female can then allow penetration.

4. The female should slowly raise one of her legs, using the male's body for support, and bring her leg over to the side so that she is now facing sideways from the male. It may help to imagine sitting on a park bench looking outwards.

5. Finally, once in position, the female can begin rocking back and forth gently or rotating her hips in a circular motion.

GOLDEN ARCH

In this position, have the male sit down with his legs straight, leaning back supporting his weight with his arms out behind him. The female should then sit on top of him and slide herself on to the penis, carefully. She should then bend her knees with her feet situated behind him and begin rocking back and forth.

1. The male should sit down with his legs out straight.

2. The male should lean backwards with his arms out straight behind him for support.

3. The female should then position herself above the male's waist and squat down for penetration. Once penetrated, she should lean back with her arms straight out behind her for support.

4. Finally, the female should position her legs behind the male by bending her knees and placing her feet towards where his hands are situated on the bed.

5. Once in position, the female can begin rocking back and forth.

This is a great position as you can both see each other's bodies and have complete control over the speed and depth of penetration.

SPIN CYCLE

This is a fun one! The male should sit on top of a washing machine with the setting that makes the most vibration. The female should saddle up on top of him, facing away and help him access the vagina.

1. First, the male should sit on top of a washing machine. The washing machine should have a load on already when trying this position!

2. The female should position herself by standing in front of the male and facing away from him.

3. The female can then begin moving backwards until she is able to saddle up on top of the male.

4. The female should help guide the penis in for penetration.

5. The male may use one arm behind him on the washing machine for support, and the other can be used to stimulate the clitoris. Alternatively, both arms can be placed behind for support.

This position gives deep penetration with the added benefit of vibrations from the washing machine! This will quickly bring you both to orgasm. If nothing else, the excitement of having sex outside of the bedroom is a great benefit in itself!

FEMALE ON TOP

The male should lay down on his back with his legs out in front of him. The female should then climb on top and let him penetrate her. She can then lean back to hold on to his ankles or come forward to get close and intimate.

1. The male should lie down on his back with his legs out in front of him.

2. The female should position herself above the male's waist and squat down for penetration. At this point, the female should transition from the squatting position to kneeling with one leg either side of the male. She should be facing towards him.

3. Once in position, the female is free to come close, sit up or lean back and place her hands on the male's feet for support and control. If she does so, she will easily be able to stimulate her clitoris herself.

This is a good one for the female as she is in control of everything. He can also have a great view of her body during sex.

THE MANHANDLE

For this position, the female should stand in front of the male and face away in a position that provides easy access for penetration. The male should then enter her (this is usually easiest when the female is bent over). She should then slowly straighten up, making sure that the penis remains inside her. When you are both ready and comfortable, start thrusting.

1. The female must start by standing in front of the male but facing away from him.

2. The female should then bend over slightly with her bottom outwards.

3. The male can then approach from behind for penetration, holding on to the female's waist for support.

4. Once inserted, the female should begin slowly standing up straighter.

5. The male can then begin thrusting.

6. The male is able to have easy access to kiss the female's neck and stimulate both the breasts and the clitoris in this position. The female is also able to

reach behind and grab the male's head to bring it forward for kissing and getting intimate.

The benefit of this position is that it can be done anytime, anywhere! With or without furniture. Inside or out. It is great on if you are able to reach orgasm through different types of stimulation.

CROSSED KEYS

The female should lay down with her bum near the edge of the bed. She should cross her legs and raise them up into the air. The male should then stand in front and penetrate her. He can then play with her legs during sex, crossing and uncrossing them to change things up a bit.

1. The female should sit on the edge of a bed with her feet on the floor.

2. The female should then lean right back until she is laid on the bed.

3. Now, the female can raise her legs and cross them. Her legs should be lifted right up into the air causing a slight elevation of her bottom.

4. The male can now approach from her front for penetration. He should hold the female's legs whilst doing so.

5. Finally, whilst having intercourse, the male should play around with her legs, crossing and uncrossing them when he pleases for different sensations.

This position can offer alterations quickly during sex to change the depth of penetration and offer different sensation. This one feels great.

MELODY MAKER

You will need a chair or something similar to start this position. To begin with, the female should sit on the chair and lean back to point her head downwards. The male should then kneel between her legs and penetrate the vagina. He should hold her hands to offer support if she needs it.

1. The female should sit down on a chair.

2. She should then lean right back until her head is pointing downwards (this might take some core strength!).

3. The male should then kneel down and approach her for penetration.

4. Once inserted, it is best to hold on to each other's hand for support and intimacy. This will also maintain stability when things get going.

The idea behind this position is that it increases the blood rush so the female can have an incredible orgasm!

THE PEG

The male should begin by laying on his side. His legs should be stretched. The female can then curl on to her side in the opposite direction so that her head is top and tail with his. She should bring her knees up to her chest and put her legs around outside his. He can then penetrate her.

1. The male should lay down on his side on a bed with his legs stretched out straight.

2. She should also lay down on her side in the same position. However, the female's head should be where the male's feet are and she should be facing him.

3. Finally, the female should curl up by bringing her knees up to her chest.

4. From this position, the male should penetrate and slowly begin thrusting.

This does seem confusing, but once you try it, it will make a lot more sense and you will soon be able to get in position in no time!

GALLOPING HORSE

The male should sit on a chair and stretch out his legs. The female should sit on top of him and slide down on to his penis. Her legs should be stretched out behind him. He should hold on to her arms to allow her to lean back. The female can then bring herself forward and back during sex.

1. The male should sit on a sturdy chair with his legs stretched out straight.

2. The female should position herself over the male facing him. She can then lower herself on to his penis for insertion.

3. Once inserted, the male should hold on to the female's hands in a firm grip.

4. Finally, the female should extend her legs out behind the male and the chair. She can then lean right back and begin thrusting back and forth.

5. Ensure that both partners are always holding on to one another's hands as the female is leaning back! She can also use this grip to launch herself forward as she reaches orgasm and wrap her arms around his shoul-

ders for intimacy and support.

This position can offer the male a great view while also giving the female deep penetration. This one is a win/ win position.

EDGE OF HEAVEN

The male should begin by sitting on the edge of a bed or on a chair. His feet should be down on the floor. The female would then climb on top of his lap with her legs either side of him. You can hold each other's hands for support and stop you from falling backwards.

1. The male should begin by sitting on the edge of a bed or on a chair.

2. The male's feet should be down on the floor.

3. The female can now, whilst facing him, mount herself on the male's lap with her legs flaying out either side of him.

4. Both partners should hold each other's hands for support so that neither fall backwards.

5. Alternatively, the female can hold on to the male's shoulders while he places his hands out behind him to support his weight.

In this position, both partners can move as slowly or as quickly as you like. It is a great one for deep penetration and G-spot stimulation. It is also a good one for staying in sync with your partner as you are both supporting each other.

REVERSE SPOONS

L ay in bed with your partner and both face the same way. He can then spoon her from behind and can begin thrusting. This is a simple position that is good for intimate sex.

1. The female should begin by laying on her side slightly curled up so that she does not lose balance.

2. The male should assume the same position from behind. Both the male and female should be facing the same way.

3. Once in position, the male can penetrate the female from behind. It may be helpful if the female raises her outer leg while he penetrates.

4. Once inserted, the male can begin thrusting. The female can also thrust back towards the male.

GOOD SPREAD

The male should lay down on his back. The female should then sit on top of him and slide down on to his penis, slowly starting to spread her legs as wide as she can.

The female is in control in this position – the wider her legs are the deeper the penetration will be.

1. The male should lie down on his back with his legs slightly apart and bent.

2. The female should position herself over the male's waist facing him. She can then squat down to allow for penetration.

3. The female should lean back slightly using her arms for support either on the bed or on the male's legs.

4. Finally, the female should open her legs as wide as possible for deeper penetration and a great view for the male.

THE BULLET

The female should lay face up on a bed and have her legs going straight up at a right angle to her body. The partner should kneel behind and start to thrust, using the upright legs as leverage. He can push the legs close together to get a better sensation inside of you, or further apart for deeper penetration.

1. The female should start by lying flat down on a bed facing the ceiling.

2. She should raise her legs up to a right angle from her body.

3. The male should then position himself in front of the female on his knees.

4. The male can then shuffle forward for penetration. It may be easier if the female slightly lifts her bottom up while this happens.

5. Finally, the male can begin thrusting.

6. Whilst having intercourse, the male can use the female's upwards legs as leverage to get harder thrusts.

He can also close her legs together whilst they are in the air so that he gets a better sensation himself.

A general rule of thumb – the wider the legs, the deeper the penetration; the tighter the legs, the better the sensation for the male!

KNEELING DOG

The female should get down on her hands and knees and lean forward on to her arms. The male can get behind in the doggy position and the female can sit back on to his lap.

1. The female should begin by getting down on her hands and knees on a bed or on the floor.

2. She should then lower her arms so that she is bent down closer to the floor. Her bottom should remain in the same position up in the air.

3. The female should slightly arch her back inwards ensuring that her bottom remains up.

4. The male can now kneel down behind her and approach her for penetration.

5. Once inserted, the female can lift her body back up slowly until she is kneeling on his lap and begin thrusting back and forth. The male has very good access for breast and clitoral stimulation in this position.

Alternatively, the female can remain with her body close to the floor and thrust in an upwards and downwards motion. It's best to mix up to two different variations during sex!

This is a great one for the male and will really get him going! It also allows for great penetration and friction with the vagina so is one of the best! You might want to write this one down...

BACK BREAKER

The female should lay on a bed with her legs off the edge as well as her bum. The male should kneel and penetrate. The female can then arch her back. The male can then thrust.

1. The female should start by sitting on the edge of a bed.

2. Next, she needs to lie right back so that her head is on the bed. A pillow should be placed under her back to create an arch.

3. The female should now shuffle forward slightly so that her bottom is now off the edge of the bed.

4. The male should now kneel down on the floor facing her. He can now grab hold of the female's bottom and penetrate.

5. The male can now thrust and should keep his hands on the female's bottom.

In this position, the male can hold on to the female's bum whilst having sex or a pillow can be used to support underneath it. The arch in the female's back is key to enhance the orgasm – it can be very easy to hit the G-spot by only making small changes in the position of the back.

PRETZEL DIP

The female should lay on her side and have her partner straddle the leg that is on the bed. The other leg should wrap around his waist.

1. The female should begin by lying down on her side on a bed.

2. The female should raise her outer leg up into the air at this point while the male gets into position.

3. The male should kneel down over the female's leg (the leg which is still on the bed).

4. The male should then shuffle forward until close to the female's waist.

5. The female should then wrap her leg (the leg in the air) around the front of the male's waist.

6. The male should then grab the leg and lift it until he is able to penetrate.

7. The male should keep hold of this leg as he begins thrusting.

G-SPOT

T he female should begin by lying on her stomach and then transitioning to face sideways in one direction. She can then bend her legs at the knee to support herself and keep balance. The male should approach her from behind on his knees for penetration. Once inserted, he may hold on to her waist while thrusting for harder and faster sex.

1. The female should start getting into a sideways position. She can bend her legs for support and balance.

2. Once in position, the male should kneel behind her and approach for penetration. It may help if the female opens her legs slightly for easier access.

3. Once inserted, the female can close her legs and the male can hold on to her hips while he thrusts.

This one, obviously, is designed to hit the G-spot! So, keep that in mind! The male does all of the work in this position and it is designed for stimulating the female orgasm so enjoy!

This is also a great position when you want to start with one thing and end with another. For example, it's very easy to transition from this position to missionary or even doggy style during sex.

SLIPPERY NIPPLE

T he male should sit upright as the female lies flat on her back. She should place her legs either side of the male and inch forward. He can then do all the work during sex. The female can lie back and enjoy.

1. The female should begin by lying down on her back facing the ceiling.

2. The female should spread her legs wide and bend them at the knee with her feet flat against the bed.

3. The male should kneel in front.

4. The female should inch forward towards the male until he is able to penetrate her.

5. Once inserted, the male has full control to lean back, but is able to lean right forward into a lowered missionary position and stimulate the nipples with his mouth hence the name.

THE CLASP

The male should begin by standing up. The female can wrap herself around his waist and he can hold her up by placing his hands on her back and bum. Allow careful penetration and the female can raise herself up and down while the male carries her.

1. This is a standing position and requires upper body strength. The male should begin by standing up. It may help for him to stand against a wall, to begin with.

2. The female should approach him facing towards him.

3. The female should wrap her arms around the male's shoulders and he should grab hold of her behind her back and under her bottom.

4. Simultaneously, the female should lift off the ground and the male should help lift her up and above his waist.

5. The male should then carefully lower the female on to his penis for penetration ensuring that he is still supporting her back and bottom.

6. Once inserted, both the male and female should help intercourse by supporting the female moving in an up and downward thrust.

If you are struggling with this position, it can be done against a wall rather than away from it. This way, the wall can support a significant portion of the female's weight and firmer thrusts can take place.

This is another position which can be done absolutely anywhere. It may require some upper body strength from the male – it can be quite hard to hold someone up for very long! It may be helpful if the female leans back against a wall or something else to support her during sex.

REVERSE COWGIRL

This is a popular classic. The male should lay down flat on his back and the female should straddle on top of him, facing away instead of towards his face. The female can then move back and forth in complete control of the pace of sex.

1. The male should lie down on a bed facing upwards. His legs should be slightly bent and slightly apart.

2. The female should position herself over the male's waist and face away from him towards his feet.

3. The female can kneel down with one leg on either side of the male's waist. She can then allow for penetration.

4. Once inserted, the female can begin thrusting back and forth.

The control from this is a great one for women and is often a popular position – some women find that they can't finish until they are on top and in control. The male benefits from having to do little work and gets a great view from behind. This can be quite a turn on.

TIGHT SQUEEZE

This is a position for adventurous sex and is best done somewhere other than the bedroom.

The female should sit down on somewhere and wrap her legs around her partner and 'tight squeeze'. The male should be standing, and the female's arms can wrap around him for support. This allows for close and intimate sex wherever you are.

1. The female should find somewhere sturdy and secure to sit up on to such as a kitchen countertop or a table.

2. The female should then shuffle close to the edge and open her legs. She may find it useful to position her hands behind her for support at this stage.

3. The male can then approach from the front and position himself between her legs for penetration.

4. Once inserted, the female should wrap her legs tightly around the male's body and squeeze, bringing him close.

5. The female can now finally also wrap her arms around the male's neck and shoulders.

6. Finally, although the male is in control during intercourse, the female is in a great position to influence the male's thrusts and movements as she pleases.

LUST AND THRUST

The female should lay down on her back off the edge of the bed with her feet on the floor. She should raise her body and support herself on her arms with elbows bent. The partner should stand in front for penetration and lean down with his arms on either side of her body.

1. The female should lie down on her back on a bed with her bottom and legs off the edge of the bed.

2. The female should raise her body from the bottom down by positioning her elbows on the bed to support her and using her arms to help lift.

3. The male should now position himself in front of the female and penetrate the female.

4. Finally, the male should lean forward and position his arms either side of the female's body during intercourse.

5. Alternatively, the male may remain standing and hold on to the female's waist while thrusting.

This position is great for getting close and intimate during sex without compromising thrust or pace. There is minimal work for the female to do during this position and both partners are well supported and secured.

AFTERNOON DELIGHT

The female should lay on her side and slightly raise her outer leg to allow easier access. The male should penetrate from the side. Once inserted, the female can relax and lower her outer leg back down to the resting position.

1. The female should begin by lying down on her side. It is best for her to maintain a slight bend in her legs at the knee.

2. The female should slightly raise her outer leg to allow easier access for penetration. It may be useful for the female to use her hands to help support her leg whilst in the air.

3. The male should approach from behind the female and shuffle into position for penetration.

4. Once inserted, the female can relax her outer leg and lower is back to the resting position.

5. The male is then free to thrust gently.

This is a good lazy position when you want to have sex, but don't have much energy!

HALF ON, HALF OFF

T he female should start by laying on a bed, legs off the end. The male can then stand and penetrate whilst the female wraps her legs around his.

1. The female should begin by lying down on the edge of the bed. Her legs should be hanging off the edge.

2. The female should open her legs outwards to allow access for the male.

3. The male can now approach from the front and position himself for penetration.

4. Once inserted, the female should lift her legs up and wrap them around the male's before having sex. If the bed is low, the male can kneel instead.

This is a good one for reaching the G-spot without having to do too much work!

THE SHIP

T he male should lay down on his back. The female should then sit down on his penis and face sideways so that both of her legs are over on one side of his body.

1. The male should begin by lying down in the basic position on a bed i.e. facing upwards, legs slightly bent and apart.

2. The female should now position herself above the waist. However, she should face to the side of the male and both feet should be next to each other on only one side of the male.

3. The female can down lower herself to allow for penetration.

4. Both of the female's legs should now be on one side of the male's body. The female may now position her hands behind her on the opposite side of the male's body for support.

This is a position where the female is in control and can be good if she needs to be on top in order to finish.

Y

The female should begin by lying face down on the bed. She should move closer to the edge so that her head and upper body hang off the bed towards to floor, using her hands for support. The male can then penetrate.

1. The female should begin by lying face down on a bed.

2. The female should now shuffle towards the edge of the bed and position herself so that her head and upper body completely hang off the edge. She may need to use her hands and arms to support her weight on the floor at this point.

3. The male should now kneel now behind the female with the aim of penetrating from behind. This is best done from a kneeling position behind her with legs either side of the female.

4. The male can now penetrate.

5. The male should help support the female's body while she is hanging off the bed. This can be done by firmly holding on to the female's waist, or by having the male hold on to the female's hands and pulling them back. This is best for when things get rough!

Again, this position is designed for the ultimate orgasm with an increased blood flow to the head and all the effort being done by the male.

THE CAT

The male lies down on top of the female in the missionary position. He then penetrates her as much as he can, bringing his body up against hers. Instead of thrusting, he can then move his hips in small circles to stimulate the clitoris with the bottom of his penis.

1. The female should begin by lying down face up on a bed with her legs slightly bent and apart.

2. The male should now position himself on top in the missionary position.

3. The male can now penetrate.

4. Once inserted, the male can push upwards into the female's body so that he is positioned slightly further up with the aim of causing more stimulation on the clitoris.

5. Finally, instead of thrusting, the male should rotate his hips in a circular motion to cause more friction on the clitoris and increase stimulation.

This is great for women who need clitoral stimulation to orgasm. Just make sure both of you are comfortable in the position. It is very easy to switch between the standard missionary position and this position, so try mixing it up!

CLOSED FOR BUSINESS

T his is an oral sex position. The female should lay down on her back with her legs 'closed for business'. The male can then go down on her.

1. The female should lie down on her back and face up-wards. Her legs should remain closed and together, but completely straight.

2. Secondly, the female should raise her hips up in to the air and position her feet behind her head as shown in the illustration.

3. The male can now kneel over her legs, facing her.

4. The male can now lean forward and begin having oral sex with the female.

This position emphasises clitoral stimulation.

HAPPY BIRTHDAY!

The male should lie down on a bed with his feet on the floor. The female should get on top with her legs either side of him and guide his penis into her vagina.

1. The male should lie down on a bed but ensure that his feet remain on the floor.

2. The female should now position herself over the male's waist a face him.

3. The female can now lower herself down to allow for penetration. Once inserted, it is best for the female to assume a kneeling position with one leg either side of the male's.

4. The female can now begin thrusting back and forth or, if she leans forward towards the chest of the male, she can thrust up and down.

The best part about this is that the female is in overall control, but the male can use his legs to help thrust and get faster when reaching climax. He also gets a great view.

ORGAN GRINDER

The female should lie on her back with her legs apart and raise them up into the air. The partner should kneel down and forward between her legs. He can then hold the legs up as he thrusts.

1. The female should lie on her back with her legs apart and bent. The female should raise her legs up into the air. She may find it helpful to use her hands to support her legs up in this position until the male is in position.

2. The male can now kneel in front of the female and move forward between her legs.

3. The male can now penetrate the female.

4. Once inserted, the male should hold on to the female's legs and keep them up in the air while he thrusts. By holding the thighs of the female, the male can use her legs to help him provide firmer thrusts.

This is a great one for reaching the G-spot and finishing sex.

THE MERMAID

F ind a surface that is flat and have the female lay down facing up with her bum at the edge. A pillow or something similar should be used to raise the hips safely and comfortably. The female should raise her legs up above and keep them closed. The male can then stand and penetrate – he can hold on to her legs to keep them secured.

1. The female should find a flat surface such as a bed, kitchen countertop or table. A pillow can be used for comfort and support.

2.
The female should raise her legs right up into the air as a 90-degree angle to her body. She should keep them closed and keep her feet together. She may use her hand to support her legs in this position until the male is in position.

3. The male can now approach from the front in a standing position and penetrate the female.

4. The male should hold on to the legs and keep them in the air and together.

5. The female can now place her hands by her side for support. Alternatively, she can place her elbows behind her and support herself from this position.

Again, keeping the legs together will cause a greater sensation for the male where there is more rubbing on the inside of the vagina. The elevation is used to make it easier to hit the G-spot.

PRETZEL

The female should lay on her side, have her partner straddle her leg and bring the other leg around his waist. This gives good penetration and the male will have his hands free for clitoral stimulation or support if needed.

1. The female should lie down on her side. Her legs should be straight at this point.

2.
The male should kneel down over the lower leg and lift the female's outer leg up while he approaches for penetration.

3.
This leg outer leg should now be wrapped around the front of the male's waist.

4.
The male can now penetrate.
5. Once inserted, the male may use his hands for support or he may stimulate the clitoris.

BACK BREAKER

The female should lie on the bed with her legs hanging off the edge. She should shift her bum forward until it is also just off the edge. The male should kneel down in front of her and penetrate. The female can push up with her toes and arch her back. The male can then hold up her bum and thrust.

1. The female should begin by lying down on a bed with her legs off the edge and her feet on the floor. She should be facing upwards.

2. The male should approach from the front for penetration.

3. Once inserted, the female should use her feet to push her body upwards and cause an arch in her back.

4. When arched, the male should grab hold of the females bottom to help her maintain the position and begin thrusting.

This position requires most effort to be done by the male, but having the female push with her toes and change the arch in her back can make it much easier to hit the G-spot.

THE BUMPER CAR

This is a thrilling sex position which allows for deep penetration. This is great if you require G-spot stimulation to reach orgasm. Again, this position requires penile flexibility, so make sure the male is comfortable with the position.

Start with the female laying down on her stomach with her legs wide open and straight out. The male should then lie down on his stomach, with his legs open and straight out. He must be facing in the opposite direction. Afterwards, the male reverses back towards his partner so his thighs are resting over hers. He needs to do this until he is able to point his penis towards his partner's vagina. Then penetrate slowly.

1. The female should lie down on her stomach facing downwards. Her legs should be open as wide as comfortably possible and straight.
2. The male should position himself facing away from the female by her feet.
3. The male should also lie down on his stomach, legs open wide and straight.
4. Once in position, the male should slowly begin moving backwards so that his thighs rest over the female's.
5. From this point, the male should focus on guiding his

penis towards the vagina and penetrate slowly, ensuring that both partners are comfortable.

6. Once inserted, the male can begin thrusting back and forth.

Safety Tips

This position requires penile flexibility. If you want to find out if the male's penis is flexible enough, have him stand against a wall. Pull his penis gradually down. If the penis is able to point directly down to the ground without causing pain then you should be fine to perform this position, but still be careful. The female should stay still when the male is initially penetrating her. The female should wait while he finds the most comfortable position and angle to thrust without injury.

BUTTER CHURNER

For this position, the female should lay on her back and bring her feet over her head so that the bum is up in the air. The male should stand over and squat up and down, coming completely out of the vagina each time.

1. The female should lie down on her back.

2. The female should bring her legs right up so that her bottom is in the air and bring her feet back over her head.

3. The male should now stand in front of the female with his feet by her bottom.

4. The male should now squat down for penetration.

5. Once inserted, the male should continue squatting up and down, penetrating and re-penetrating the female each time.

This position will feel like the male is penetrating for the first time every time he penetrates which can be really satisfying.

KNEEL AND SIT

The male should kneel on a bed and the female should straddle him with her legs either side. The female has to control and choice in this position – sit, grind or move up and down. It's up to you!

1. The male should begin by kneeling on a bed or anywhere else that seems comfortable.

2. The female should approach the male from the front and straddle his lap with one leg on either side of the male. The female should be on her feet rather than on her knees and should be facing away from the male.

3. The female can then position herself to allow for penetration.

The male has good access to the female's upper body in this position.

WRAPAROUND

The male should sit on a floor with his legs out. The female should straddle and wrap her legs around him and carefully allow him to penetrate her.

1. The male should sit down on the floor with his legs out in front of him.

2. The female should position herself above the male, facing him and with one foot either side of the male's legs.

3. The female can now lower herself to allow for penetration.

4. Once inserted, the female should wrap her legs around the back of the male.

5. For support, the male can either wrap his arms around the female or lean back on his arms.

This position is great as it gives some control back to the male. You are able to stay close and kiss whilst having sex without compromising the amount of penetration.

THE LANDSLIDE

The female should begin by laying down looking at the floor. She should rest upon her forearms with her legs apart. The partner should sit behind and over her legs, also leaning back on his arms behind him. He should then penetrate and begin having sex.

1. The female should start by lying face down on the floor.

2. The female places her forearms below her chest and rest on them. Her legs should also be apart at this point.

3. The male should then sit behind the female on his knees. His legs should be over hers and on both sides i.e. outside of her legs.

4. The male can now position himself to allow for penetration.

5. Once inserted, the male should lean back on his hands with his arms stretched out behind him.

By having the female close her legs, the male will feel fuller inside and it is much easier to find the G-spot.

LAP

T his is a simple position. The male should sit up, using a wall or headboard to support him. The female sits on top and both can rock together.

1. The male should sit up in front of a wall or a headboard with his legs crossed.

2. The female can now position herself facing towards the male and above his lap.

3. The female should now lower herself in a squat to allow for penetration. She can remain with her feet on the floor or on her knees.

4. Once inserted, the female is in control and can rock back and forth.

This is a good position for a long sex session.

HOME FITNESS

In this position, both the male and female get into the push-up position. The female should be on the bottom and can use her knees to support. The male penetrates her from behind. This is a VERY exhausting position but can be worth the effort!

1. The female should begin by getting into a press-up position. She may find it easier to rest on her knees.

2. The male should position himself over the female in the press-up position.

3. The male should carefully penetrate the female – he may use one of his arms to help penetrate if he has the strength to hold up his weight on one arm.

SHOULDER STAND

The female should start by being on her back and the male should kneel in front. She should wrap her legs around and allow him to penetrate. He supports her with one hand on her back and she can then shift all her weight on to her shoulders. He can now thrust.

1. The female should begin by lying down on her back with her legs open and slightly bent.

2. The male should kneel in front of the female and move towards her to allow for penetration.

3. Once inserted, the female should wrap her legs tightly around the male's back and bottom.

4. The male should now place either one or both hands on the female's back to support her.

5. The female can now lift her back until all of her weight is supported by her shoulders. She should maintain this arch position throughout intercourse.

The be secure and safe, the male should always provide support to the female.

This position allows for very deep penetration and incredible orgasms.

DINNER TIME

The female should sit on a sofa on the edge. The partner should kneel in front and be between her legs. He can hold her thighs to get some more control as he engages in oral sex.

1. The female should sit straight up on the edge of a sofa. Alternatively, she can lean back flat.

2. The male should kneel in front of the female and take hold of her thighs.

3. The male should spread the female's legs wide and engage in oral sex.

4. The female should relax her legs so that the male has full control of their position throughout oral sex. If she resists or has impulses, the male should restrain her from moving – he is in control!

FACE SITTER

This is an oral sex position – the name says it all here!

The male should lay down on his back. The female should lower herself above his face. Do NOT put all your weight down – the female should support herself using a wall or the bed. The female is in complete control of where his tongue is going.

1. The male should lack down on his back.

2. The female should position herself over the male's head facing either way.

3. The female can now squat down until the male is able to begin oral sex.

4. The female must remember to support all of her weight throughout this position. She is in total control of how the male's mouth is positioned and what it does.

THE THIGH MASTER

This position is a variation of the cowgirl position. To begin with, the female should be on top facing away from the male. The male's knees should be raised to give the female something to support her.

1. The male should lie down in his back with his legs apart and slightly bent.

2. The female should position herself above his waist and face towards him.

3. The female can now kneel down with one leg either side of the male to allow for penetration.

4. Once inserted, the male should bend his legs further whilst keeping his feet firmly flat on the bed.

5. The female should rest back against the male's bent legs as she uses her hips only to thrust back and forth.

Being on top is generally great for the female orgasm, but having the male's knees up will make his sensation better inside the female and you can both have a better orgasm together.

THE STAIRCASE

The female should sit on some stairs with her back leaning against one of the walls. The male should be standing a bit further down. The female should lift one leg up as the male penetrates her. He can then begin thrusting.

Just make sure no one else is around!

1. Locate an appropriate staircase!

2. Have the female sit on the staircase several steps up from the male. This will depend on the height of both partners so you may need to find what is most comfortable for you both.

3. The female should lift one of her legs up on to the male's shoulders and rest them there throughout this position.

4. The male can then penetrate, using the female's raised leg for support and to aid with firmer thrusts.

KNEELING WHEELBARROW

This one is easier than the one we tried earlier! The female starts off on all fours, putting her weight on to one forearm and one knee. The partner then kneels down behind and penetrates the vagina. This is another great one for hitting to G-spot.

1. The female should start by getting down on her hands and knees.

2. The female should then move on to her forearms instead of on her hands.

3. The female should now rest all of her weight on to one of her forearms and one of her knees on the same side.

4. The male should now kneel behind the female and penetrate, holding on to both of the female's upper legs when thrusting.

DINNER IS SERVED

The female should wrap her legs around her partner and have him hold her bum in a carrying position. He should then penetrate. The female can then begin to lean back until parallel to the floor.

1. The male should begin by standing in front of the female.

2. The female should then, holding on to the male's shoulders, jump up and wrap her legs around the back of the male. Think of this as a carrying position.

3. The female should then allow for penetration.

4. Once inserted, the male should grab a firm hold of the female's hands and allow her to lean right back until her body is parallel to the floor.

5. The female can now begin using her legs to help her thrust up and down.

This position is really fun and for both partners. It does require some upper body strength though! If this position is too difficult in terms of strength required, the female can rest her back on a bed instead of being elevated in the air parallel to the ground.

BALLET

This is an exhaustive position that requires flexibility, stamina and strength from both partners. Rather than a unique sex position, this is better thought of as an exciting way to begin having sex.

The female must begin by standing on a surface close to other structures that can be used for support such as a wall or cabinet. She should then lunge forward and lower herself, while the male does the same. He should inch closer in order to penetrate. Either party can now control the depth of penetration for the best orgasm.

1. The female should begin by standing on a surface which is close to other firm surroundings such as walls or heavy/ fitted furniture.

2. The male should be standing in front of her.

3. Once in position, the male should ready himself to catch the female and support all of her body weight.

4. The female should lunge forward towards the male. He should be ready to support her. It is best for the male to catch the female by holding her under the shoulders. When caught, she should be positioned around the male's shoulder area.

5. The male can then lower the female while she keeps

her legs out straight to the sides.

6. Penetration can then take place.

Balance is key! Be sure to use surrounding supports in case!

LEG UP!

Y ou should both begin by facing each other. The female should raise one leg up and wrap it around the male's leg, pulling him closer.

1. Both the male and female should begin by standing and facing one another.

2. The female should raise one leg up and bend it at the knee.

3. The female should then use her leg and wrap it around the male's. She can then use her leg to bring him closer for penetration to take place.

4. The female should keep her leg wrapped around the male for the entirety of this position.

This is great when you can't find a bedroom to have sex or just want to mix things up a bit!

DIRTY DANCING

This is another anywhere, anytime move but the support of a sturdy object may be helpful when you haven't tried it before.

The male should lean on a wall facing the female and hold her. She should straddle him and wrap her legs around for balance.

1. The male should lean back against a wall, facing the female.

2. The female should hop up on to the male and wrap her legs around his back. He should use his hands to support her from the bottom.

3. The female should now allow for penetration.

4. Once inserted, the female can use the male's shoulders to help her move up and down during sex.

This is an intimate position where the male has a lot of access to the female's upper body. The penetration and clitoral stimulation can be controlled easily.

LEAPFROG

L eapfrog is very much like the doggy style position that was covered earlier in this book – it is a variation of the doggy position.

For this position, you should start in the typical doggy style pose, but the female should lower her head and arms so that they are resting on the bed. The partner should then continue to penetrate from behind like usual.

1. The female should begin by getting down on her hands and knees facing away from the male.

2. The female should then lower her upper body by transitioning from resting on her hands to resting on her forearms. Her bottom should remain up in the air and she should arch her back inwards.

3. The male should kneel behind the female, just like the doggy style, and approach for penetration.

4. The male can then thrust firmly.

The great thing about this position is that penetration becomes much deeper than usual and it also frees up the hands. It is also great for getting a bit rougher than the normal doggy style positions.

69

This is perhaps one of the wider known and popular foreplay positions. For this, the male should lay down facing upwards. The female should straddle on top facing the male's feet end. She should stretch out on top of the male and begin oral sex, while he does the same.

1. The male should begin by lying down on his back on a bed and face upwards. His legs should be slightly apart, but straight.

2. The female should then position herself by kneeling over the stomach of the male with one leg either side. She should be facing away towards the male's feet.

3. The female can then begin shuffling backwards until her waist is position above the male's face for oral sex.

4. The male can then engage in oral sex.

5. The female can now lean forward so that her face is above the male's waist. She can then also engage in oral sex at the same time as the male.

Both partners benefit from this position and can be great for stimulation before having sex.

THE HINGE

The male should begin by kneeling upon a bed and leaning back to support his own weight. The female should face away, positioned in the doggy pose. She should lean down on to her forearms and move backwards until he has penetrated and begin having sex. This is good for keeping control of the penetration and speed.

1. The male should begin by kneeling on a bed and leaning backwards. He should position his arms behind him to help support his weight in this position.

2. The female should then face away from the male in front of him. She should get into the doggy style position i.e. on her hand and knees.

3. The female should lean forward on to her forearms and raise her bottom.

4. The female can now shuffle back towards the male to allow for penetration.

5. Both the male and female can thrust up and down in this position.

THE MISSIONARY 180

This position puts a spin on the traditional missionary position, but it requires the male to be flexible!

First, the female needs to lay down on her back with her legs spread apart. The male then lies on top, but with his head down towards her feet – his legs should then be on either side of her body. Once in position, the male should carefully push his penis downwards and penetrate his partner. Get comfortable and perform upward and downward thrusts.

1. The female should lie down on her back facing upwards.

2. The male should then position himself on top of the female, but with his head towards her feet. The male should be using his arms to bear his weight at this point or, alternatively, be resting his weight on his elbows.

3. The male must now position his legs either side of the female if not done so already.

4. The male should now slowly lower his middle section and begin pushing his penis back and towards the vagina. The female may help guide the penis while the male supports his weight.

5. Once inserted, the male can begin upward and downward thrusts.

Safety Tips

This position requires the male to have a very flexible penis – make sure he is comfortable before committing to the position! There is a risk of him straining his penis's suspensory ligaments. If he does feel any significant pain you should consider leaving the position behind and finding something better suited and comfortable. When entering the position, the female should be careful not to pull hard on the penis while guiding it inside her.

Looking for more sex positions? Check out
*"101 Sex Positions to Make Her Scream – **FULLY
ILLUSTRATED**"* by Madeleine Carter
on the Kindle Store for 101 fully illustrated
sex positions with pictures. Also available
as paperback.

A second edition title by **Madeleine Carter**

Printed in Great Britain
by Amazon